How to Export and Import

Michael E. Allen

Lotus Press
4735/22, Prakash Deep Building,
Ansari Road, Daryaganj,
New Delhi - 110002

Lotus Press Publishers & Distributors
Unit No.220, 2nd Floor, 4735/22, Prakash Deep Building,
Ansari Road, Daryaganj, New Delhi- 110002
Ph:- 32903912, 23280047, 098118-38000
Email : lotuspress1984@gmail.com
Visit us : www.lotuspress.co.in

How to Export and Import

ISBN : 978-81-8382-018-9

Printed & Published by : **Lotus Press Publishers & Distributors,** New Delhi- 2

How to
Export and Import

Published by
Lotus Press Publishers & Distributors

PREFACE

This book brings you completely up-to-date guidance on every aspect of conceiving, launching, and operating a successful import/export business. It covers every aspects to run an import/export business: how to start an import/export business, how to develop an export strategy, how to sell overseas, how to collect money from overseas transactions, how to face the legal issues in import/export, and so on. It is an essential reading for anyone concerned with importing and exporting. It will help the reader to become a key player in the glamorous and lucrative world of international business.

Editor

This book brings you completely up-to-date guidance on every aspect of conceiving, launching, and operating a successful import/export business. It covers every aspects to run an import/export business: how to start an import/export business, how to develop an export strategy, how to sell overseas, how to collect money from overseas transactions, how to face the legal issues in import/export, and so on. It is an essential reading for anyone concerned with importing and exporting. It will help the reader to become a key player in the glamorous and lucrative world of international business.

CONTENTS

1

HOW TO START AN IMPORT/ EXPORT BUSINESS

In this new century international trade is one of the hot industriy. Importing is not just for those lone footloose adventurer types who survive by their wits and the skin of their teeth. Exporting is just as big. Everything from beverages to commodes—and a staggering list of other products you might never imagine as global merchandise—are fair game for the savvy trader. And these products are bought, sold, represented and distributed somewhere in the world on a daily basis.

But the import/export field is not the sole purview of the conglomerate corporate trader, the big guys make up only about 4 percent of all exporters. Which means that the other 96 percent of exporters—the lion's share are small outfits like yours wil be—when you're new, at least.

Import is a big business around the world. Three main reasons are:

1. *Availability*: There are some things you just can't grow or make in your home country. Bananas in Alaska, for example, mahogany lumber in Maine, or Ball Park franks in France.

2. *Cachet*: A lot of things, like caviar and champagne, pack more cachet, more of an "image," if they're imported rather than home-grown. Think Scandinavian furniture, German beer, French perfume, Egyptian cotton. Even when you can make it at home, it all seems classier when it comes from distant shores.
3. *Price*: Some products are cheaper when brought in from out of the country. Korean toys, Taiwanese electronics and Mexican clothing, to rattle off a few, can often be manufactured or assembled in foreign factories for far less money than if they were made on the domestic front.

Aside from cachet items, countries typically export goods and services that they can produce inexpensively and import those that are produced more efficiently somewhere else. What makes one product less expensive for a nation to manufacture than another? Two factors: resources and technology. A country with extensive oil resources and the technology of a refinery, for example, will export oil but may need to import clothing.

1.1. TYPES OF IMPORT/EXPORT BUSINESSES

First off, let's take a look at the players. While you've got your importers and your exporters, there are many variations on the main theme:

1. *Export management company (EMC)*: An EMC handles export operations for a domestic company that wants to sell its product overseas but doesn't know how (and perhaps doesn't want to know how). The EMC does it all—hiring dealers, distributors and representatives; handling advertising, marketing and promotions; overseeing marking and packaging; arranging shipping; and

sometimes arranging financing. In some cases, the EMC even takes title to the goods, in essence becoming its own distributor. EMCs usually specialise by product, foreign market or both, and—unless they've taken title—are paid by commission, salary or retainer plus commission.

2. *Export trading company (ETC)*: While an EMC has merchandise to sell and is using its energies to seek out buyers, an ETC attacks the other side of the trading coin. It identifies what foreign buyers want to spend their money on and then hunts down domestic sources willing to export. An ETC sometimes takes title to the goods and sometimes works on a commission basis.
3. *Import/export merchant*: This international entrepreneur is a sort of free agent. He has no specific client base, and he doesn't specialise in any one industry or line of products. Instead, he purchases goods directly from a domestic or foreign manufacturer and then packs, ships and resells the goods on his own. This means, of course, that unlike the EMC, he assumes all the risks.

1.2. TRADE CHANNEL

Now that you're familiar with the players, you'll need to take a swim in the trade channel, the means by which the merchandise travels from manufacturer to end user. A manufacturer who uses a middleman who resells to the consumer is paddling around in a three-level channel of distribution. The middleman can be a merchant who purchases the goods and then resells them, or he can be an agent who acts as a broker but doesn't take title to the stuff. Who your fellow swimmers are will depend on how you configure your trade channel, but they could include any of the following:

1. *Manufacturer's representative*: A salesperson who specialises in a type of product or line of complementary products; for example, home electronics: televisions, radios, CD players and sound systems. He often provides additional product assistance, such as warehousing and technical service.
2. *Distributor or wholesale distributor*: A company that buys the product you've imported and sells it to a retailer or other agent for further distribution until it gets to the end user.
3. *Representative*: A savvy salesperson who pitches your product to wholesale or retail buyers, then passes the sale on to you; differs from a manufacturer's representative in that he doesn't necessarily specialise in a particular product or group of products.
4. *Retailer*: The tail end of the trade channel where the merchandise smacks into the consumer; as yet another variation on a theme, if the end user is not Joan Q. Public but an original equipment manufacturer (OEM), then you don't need to worry about the retailer because the OEM becomes your end of the line.

Not everybody is cut out to be an international trader. This is not, for example, a career for the sales-phobic. If you're one of those people who would rather work on a chain gang than sell Girl Scout cookies, or if you blanch at the thought of making a sales pitch, then you don't want to be in import/export. This is also not a career for the organisationally challenged. If you're one of those let-the-devil-handle-the-details types whose idea of follow-up is waiting to see what happens next, you should think twice about international trading.

If, on the other hand, you're an enthusiastic salesperson, a dynamo at tracking things like invoices and shipping receipts, and your idea of heaven is seeing where new ideas and new products will take you, and if, to top it off, you love the excitement of dealing with people from different cultures, then this is the career for you. It also helps if you already have a background in import/export.

Every business needs consumers for its products and services to, as the Vulcans so eloquently put it, live long and prosper. Now that you know what running an import/export business entails, you need to plan, or target, your market, and determine who your potential clients will be, which geographic areas you'll draw from, and what specific products or services you'll offer to draw them in. This is a very important phase in the mega-trader building project. The proper market research can help boost your trading company into a true profit center, and the more research you do, the better prepared you are before you officially open your doors, the less floundering you're likely to do.

1.3. CUSTOMERS

Any manufacturer, supplier, crafter, artisan, importer, exporter or retailer is fair game. You can go after companies that deal in heavy construction equipment or delicate jewelry, gourmet goodies or pet food, telecommunications or toys. The only essential requirement is that they want to sell their merchandise or buy someone else's. This doesn't mean, however, that your best technique is standing at manufacturers' gates, tripping them as they walk to their cars after work each evening. Targeting by definition means homing in on a specific group.

If you have previous experience in a particular field, for example, you should seriously consider targeting that market first. You'll feel comfortable with the jargon and procedures so your sales pitch—and your initial sales—will go smoother and easier. As an added bonus, you may already have contacts in the field who can either become your first clients or steer you to colleagues in that area.

1.4. INTERNATIONAL MARKETING STRATEGIES

As an international trader, your mission is sales—in two different but overlapping arenas:

1. Selling yourself and your company to clients as an import/export manager for their products, and
2. Selling the products themselves to representatives and distributors.

Success in one of these arenas will contribute to your success in another. Once you've established a favorable sales record with one client's goods, you'll have a track record with which to entice other clients. And, of course, each success will contribute to your own self-confidence, which will, in turn, lend that air of confidence to your negotiations with new prospects.

A surprisingly small percentage of domestic producers export their wares. So your marketing goal is to convince the huge remainder that they can increase profits by exporting—with your guidance—to specific target countries. You can accomplish this with direct mail and cold calls. If you're starting with imports, don't ignore this section—you'll work in basically the same manner. Before you initiate contact with any manufacturer, you'll need to do some basic market research:

1. What products are hot sellers in the domestic marketplace? Focus your attention on products that you know well or use yourself, or that are bestsellers in their market niches.
2. Are these products hot sellers in your target countries?
3. If not, are there situations or markets that would put these products in great demand if the products were available?
4. Who manufactures these products?
5. What is the selling price of each product—and of competing products or brands—domestically and in your target countries?

1.4.1. Direct-Mail Campaign

Now you're ready to begin your direct-mail campaign. Choose one manufacturer of one of the products you've researched. Then call the company and ask for the name of the person to whom you'll want to write. If the company is small, you'll probably want the president or owner. If it's a larger concern, you might want to direct your letter to the vice president in charge of sales, the sales manager or the president or owner. Armed with a name and title, write your letter, taking care to address the following points.

1. Introduce yourself and your company.
2. Briefly outline the potential of the overseas market.
3. Outline the product's potential within that market.
4. If possible, explain why and how your company, out of all others, will be able to position the product best. For example, if you have experience with like products, be sure to say so.

5. If you already have contacts with foreign distributors, explain that you have foreign representatives for overseas sales.
6. Ask for a personal meeting to further discuss the possibilities.

Once your first letter is in the mail, sit down and write another to a potential client in another product line. And then another, until you've exhausted your first set of preliminary market research products. Now wait a week or 10 days. If you haven't heard from your first target manufacturer, give him a call. Ask to set up a meeting in his office to discuss your plan.

Then call the next manufacturer and the next. If you're not familiar with sales, you may find this portion of the programme a white-knuckler. Don't be nervous! You're offering these people a terrific opportunity. Not everyone is going to bite (not everyone can recognise a great deal when it jumps up and grabs them), but not everyone is going to turn you down, either. A no thank you now and then is part of the game.

1.4.2. Cold-Calling

Cold-calling, so-called because you call a potential client "cold" without any warming up by prior contact, is an alternative to the direct-mail approach. The good news is that, if you're calling locally, it's usually cheaper than direct mail. The bad news is that it requires much more perseverance to be effective. The other good news, however, is that, done properly, a cold call can be much more effective than direct mail. Before you make your first call, be sure you know what you want to say and how you want to say it.

Some experts recommend writing out a sort of "script" that you can follow during the course of your call. This is a good starting-off exercise to help plan your spiel, but be aware of the fact that following a script has its drawbacks. The main one is that the person you're calling doesn't know he's supposed to be following the script, too, and when he gets off track, so do you.

How do you go about finding goods to bring stateside? You have several options:

1. Travel abroad on an import search mission.
2. Wait for foreign manufacturers to contact you.
3. Attend trade shows.
4. Contact foreign embassies' trade development offices.
5. Contact the U.S. Department of Commerce's International Trade Association.
6. Track down leads on the Internet and in trade publications.

1.4.3. Marketing Plan

Whether you're planning on exporting or importing, be prepared to present your prospective client with a marketing plan. If the manufacturer is close to home, you'll naturally present it in person. If she's overseas, you may still have to (make that get to) arrange a personal visit to close the deal. If you feel strongly enough about the product's U.S. potential, the trip will be worth the time and expense. To prepare your marketing plan, you'll need the information you've already asked for: pricing, product brochures or literature, and samples.

If your prospect balks at supplying these materials, tell her that you'll need them to further explore the market potential and develop a presentation for her, outlining the market strategy you plan to pursue. Once you have the materials in your office, sit down and figure out every possible expense you'll have so you can arrive at your sales price. Then, if you've already been in ntact with distributors or representatives, find out if 's price will sell in their market. If you don't have any ..presentatives yet, you'll need to locate one and determine if he can work with that price. Assuming the answer is yes, you've got a viable product. Now write out your marketing plan, which should include the following elements:

1. *Target*: Which country or countries will you or your representatives sell in? Why are these markets viable? Include positive market research information and be sure to assemble it in a clear, concise, easy-to-digest format. This is where your desktop publishing programmes will shine—you can make charts, graphs and tables interspersed with facts, figures and text.
2. *Sales*: Explain at what price you'll sell the product, give your annual sales forecast, your fee structure and the profits the manufacturer can expect.
3. *Marketing*: Briefly touch on any special marketing or promotions for the product; for example, foreign or domestic trade shows or any local advertising your reps will do.

1.5. MARKET RESEARCH

Here's a rapid-fire overview of your market research tasks. You'll want to do some in-depth investigation into each of these areas:

1. The product or service you'll sell.
2. The end user you'll aim for (mass-market consumer, heavy industry, light industry, medical or hospital use, government, business or professional).

3. The country or countries you'll export to or import from.
4. The trade channel you'll use (direct sales, representative, distributor or commission representative).

One of the catch-22s of being in business for yourself is that you need money to make money—in other words, you need startup funds. These costs range from less than $5,000 to more than $25,000 for the import/export business. You can start out homebased, which means you won't need to worry about leasing office space. You don't need to purchase a lot of inventory, and you probably won't need employees. Your basic necessities will be a computer, printer, fax machine and modem. If you already have these items, then you're off and running.

One of the many nifty things about an import/export business is that its startup costs are comparatively low. You have the advantage of homebased-ability, which cuts office lease expenses down to nothing. Unless you're starting as a distributor, you can get away with purchasing no inventory, which means no outlay of funds for pretty doodads to grace display spaces (you have no display spaces!). Your major financial outlay will go toward office equipment and market research expenses—and if you're like many moderns, you already have the most expensive piece of office equipment: a computer system.

But let's take it from the top. The following is a breakdown of everything—from heavy investment pieces to flyweight items—you'll need to get up and running:

1. Computer system with modem and printer,
2. Fax machine,
3. Internet/e-mail service,
4. Software,

5. Market research and/or trade leads,
6. Phone,
7. Voice mail or answering machine,
8. Stationery and office supplies,
9. Postage,
10. Travel expenses for conducting market research on foreign turf.

You can add all kinds of goodies of varying degrees of necessity to this list. For example, a copier is a plus. It's also nice to have bona fide office furniture: a tweedy upholstered chair with lumbar support that swivels and rolls, gleaming file cabinets that really lock, real oak bookshelves.

But let's consider that you're starting from scratch. You can always set up your computer on your kitchen table or on a card table in a corner of the bedroom. You can stash files in cardboard boxes. It's not glamorous, but it'll suffice until you get your business steaming ahead.

What can you expect to make as an international trader? The amount's entirely up to you, depending only on how serious you are and how willing you are to expand. Some traders work from home, supplementing 9-to-5 incomes with their trading expertise. Others have launched thriving full-time businesses that demand constant care and feeding.

1.6. PRICING STRUCTURE

As an international trader, you're an intermediary in the buying and selling, or importing and exporting, transaction. Therefore, you have to determine not just the price of the product, but the price of your services as well. These two figures are separate yet interactive.

Because you're a swimmer in the trade channel, the price of your services has to be added on to the product price, and that can affect its competitiveness in the marketplace. Since the fee for your services will impact the success of the product, you may ultimately decide to change your pricing structure.

You don't want to undercharge your client so that you can't cover your expenses and make a profit, but you don't want to overcharge and reduce the competitiveness of your company and the merchandise you represent. Import/export management companies use two basic methods to price their services: commission and retainer. Normally, you choose one method or the other based on how salable you feel the product is. If you think it's an easy sell, you'll want to work on the commission method. If you feel it's going to be an upstream swim, difficult to sell and require a lot of market research, you'll ask for a retainer.

A third method is to purchase the product outright and sell it abroad. This is a common scenario when you're dealing with manufacturers who would rather use you as a distributor than as a representative. You'll still market the product under the manufacturer's name, but your income will come from the profit generated by sales rather than by commission. Import/export management companies usually operate on a commission basis of about 10 percent. These fees are based on the product cost from the manufacturer.

If the manufacturer can't discount her price sufficiently or if you feel that the product will be a tough sell, you'll want to ask for a flat retainer (the monetary kind, not the dental appliance kind). You'll pass all the costs of market research along to the manufacturer. By taking a retainer, you guarantee yourself a set income rather than one tied by commission to a "problem" product. To determine what your retainer should be, you'll need to consider three variables associated with the performance of your services:

1. *Labour and materials or supplies*: This usually includes your salary or estimated salary on an hourly basis plus the wages and benefits you pay any employees involved in the performance of the job. To determine labour costs, estimate the amount of time it will take to finish a job and multiply it by the hourly rate of your salary and that of any employees you might use. You can compute materials as a percentage of labour, but until you have past records to use as a guide, you should use 2 to 6 percent.
2. *Overhead*: This variable comprises all the nonlabour, indirect expenses required to operate your business. To determine your overhead rate, add up all your expenses for one year, except for labour and materials. Divide this figure by your total cost of labour and materials to determine your overhead rate. Or use a rate of 35 percent to 42 percent of your labour and materials.
3. *Profit*: And the end result is: After all labour, materials and overhead expenses are deducted, profit can be determined by applying a percentage profit factor to the combined costs of labour and materials and overhead.

What you will be doing during your peak hours and beyond will depend upon how you've structured your services. Some traders act only as sales representatives, finding buyers and taking commissions, but steer clear of the shipping, documentation and financing aspects of the deal. Others are happier offering a full line of services, buying directly from the manufacturer and taking on all the responsibilities of transactions from shipping to marketing. These traders often specialise in either import or export and stick to the merchandise industry they know best. No matter how exotic you want to get, your most basic tasks will be obtaining merchandise, selling it, transporting it and getting paid for it.

1.6.1. The export path

Exporter—you've found a buyer for your merchandise. You're a player. You're ready to roll. So now what do you do? Follow the export path:

1. Generate the pro forma invoice—give the importer a quote on your merchandise; negotiate if necessary.
2. Receive the letter of credit from your bank.
3. Fulfill terms of the letter of credit: Have the merchandise manufactured if necessary; make shipping and insurance arrangements; pack the merchandise; and have the merchandise transported.
4. Collect shipping documents.
5. Present shipping documents to your bank.

1.6.2. The import path

You've found the merchandise you want to buy and then resell. You're a player. You're ready to roll. So now what do you do? Follow the import path:

1. Receive the pro forma invoice, the exporter's quote on the merchandise; negotiate if necessary.
2. Open a letter of credit at your bank.
3. Verify that the merchandise has been shipped.
4. Receive documents from the exporter.
5. See merchandise through customs.
6. Collect your merchandise.

2

DEVELOPING AN EXPORT STRATEGY

More and more small business owners are paying attention to the unlimited potential of the growing, global economy. There was a time when exporting products to foreign countries was simply not practical for most small businesses. But today, exporting your products may be just the ticket for your company.

2.1. THINGS TO CONSIDER BEFORE EXPORTING YOUR PRODUCTS

Here are some things to consider before you decide to send your products abroad.

1. *Domestic sales*: The first question you need to ask is whether or not your products are selling domestically. Exporting is not a panacea to boost sagging sales. If your products aren't selling here, then they probably won't sell anywhere else, either.
2. *Exportability*: Next, you'll need to decide if your products are "exportable". Do your products fill a niche that is exclusive to the market? Are they packaged in a way that can be understood by the consumers? Do they violate cultural taboos or contain ingredients that are prohibitive to their sale in a foreign context?

3. *Foreign partnerships*: Once you have decided that your products are both saleable and exportable, you'll need to find foreign partners who are willing to either purchase or distribute your products.

Unless you are planning to establish a retail operation of foreign soil, you are going to have to establish business to business sales relationships. You can either sell your products directly to foreign retailers or to foreign distributors who sell to those retailers. A secondary advantage of establishing foreign relationships is that your foreign partners will be able to provide you with valuable, local insight about import regulations, product marketability, and local customs. Even though establishing foreign relationships can be difficult, you do have several resources at your disposal.

2.2. DEVELOPING AN EXPORT PLAN

Once you have decided to sell your products abroad, it is time to develop an export plan. A crucial first step in planning is to develop broad consensus among key management on the company's goals, objectives, capabilities, and constraints. In addition, all aspects of an export plan should be agreed upon by the personnel involved in the exporting process, as they will ultimately execute the export plan. The purposes of the export plan are:

1. To assemble facts, constraints, and goals and
2. To create an action statement that takes all of these into account.

The statement includes specific objectives, it sets forth time schedules for implementation, and it marks milestones so that the degree of success can be measured and help motivate personnel.

The first time an export plan is developed, it should be kept simple. It need be only a few pages long, since important market data and planning elements may not yet be available. The initial planning effort itself gradually generates more information and insight. As the planners learn more about exporting and your company's competitive position, the export plan will become more detailed and complete. From the start, the plan should be viewed and written as a management tool, not as a static document. Objectives in the plan should be compared with actual results to measure the success of different strategies. The company should not hesitate to modify the plan and make it more specific as new information and experience are gained.

2.3. LEGAL ISSUES INVOLVED IN EXPORTING

The last step in establishing an export component for your business is to research the legal issues involved in exporting your products to certain parts of the world. Some products, such as technology and agricultural products, are subject to severe export limitations. There may also be import restrictions depending on the countries you are dealing with.

Additionally, the post 9/11 world has created heightened sensitivities about exporting products that can even remotely be used in a military or terrorist capacity. Since you can't possibly be aware of all the restrictions and licensing requirements you may or may not be facing, your best advice is to consult an attorney specialising in international law to make sure you are in compliance with the appropriate domestic and foreign regulations.

There are several ways to evaluate the export potential of your products and services in overseas markets. The most common approach is to examine the success of your products domestically. If your company succeeds at selling in the market, there is a good chance that it will also be successful in markets abroad, at least those where similar needs and conditions exist. Another means to assess your company's potential in exporting is by examining the unique or important features of your product.

If those features are hard to duplicate abroad, then it is likely that you will be successful overseas. A unique product may have little competition and demand for it might be quite high. Finally, your product may have export potential even if there are declining sales in market. Sizeable export markets may still exist, especially if the product once did well, but is now losing market share to more technically advanced products. Other countries may not need state-of-the-art technology and/or may be unable to afford the most sophisticated and expensive products. Such markets may have a surprisingly healthy demand for products that are older or considered obsolete by market standards.

2.4. DON'TS OF EXPORTING

This section describes how you can quality control your export operations. Following are some of the "don'ts"of exporting.

Don't-1: Don't assume that export controls relevant to your product at any one time will remain relevant forever. Export controls, which take the form of export prohibitions and various export license requirements, result from government's action related to concerns over national security, foreign policy and short supply. Consequently, as government's concern over these matters shifts, export controls will likely be subject to change. Violations export control laws have many serious repercussions, ranging from denial of export privileges and product seizure through monetary fines to imprisonment.

Don't-2: Don't forget that you as an exporter are responsible for complying with all export control laws that are relevant to your product. Such responsibility makes you liable for your own actions, as well as for the actions of your agents and customers.

Thus, if any export prohibition or any export license requirement exists with regard to your product, you are responsible for preventing your agents and customers from re-exporting your products in violation of such prohibition or requirement. The penalties that attach to a violation of export control law by your agents or customers are the same as the penalties you would incur, had you committed the export control law infraction yourself.

Don't-3: Don't neglect to investigate whether the foreign market into which you are exporting your product has any import controls related to the sale of your product. Import controls breakdown into import prohibitions, import restrictions (quotas) and import licensing requirements. They may be based on country of origin, product type, or product characteristics, such as products produced by convicts and counterfeit products. Imported products which contravene an importing country's import controls are generally refused entry at the importing country's border.

Don't- 4: Don't assume that you can sell your products into foreign markets without making any alterations to your products. Many foreign markets attempt to discourage imports by subjecting imported products to various "special requirements". These "special requirements" generally fall into the following categories:

1. Product specifications, product testing requirements or product certification requirements.

2. Marking requirements dealing with country of origin and the country's unique definition of country of origin.
3. Labeling requirements.
4. Packaging requirements.
5. Documentary requirements.

Imported products which do not comply with an importing country's "special requirements" may be refused entry into the importing country, seized at the border, assessed a monetary penalty or subjected to a programme of forced compliance.

Don't-5: Don't ignore your responsibilities with regard to the export laws that mandate against certain types of behavior.

Don't pay, offer to pay or promise to pay any commissions to a foreign official or to relatives or friends of a foreign official for the purpose of closing a deal.

Don't knowingly or inadvertently participate in another country's boycott of a country friendly to your country. This type of activity is contrary to the government's anti-boycott law which subjects companies that violate the act to penalties ranging from denial of export privileges through monetary fines to imprisonment.

Don't-6: Don't neglect to evaluate country risk in addition to buyer risk in selecting the proper payment method for your export transactions. Countries frequently experience political and economic problems so severe that buyers in such countries are precluded from obtaining the necessary foreign currency to pay for their imports. Exporters that ship to such countries without having investigated the country's political and economic situation and without having selected a payment method appropriate in light of such political and economic situation run the risk of not receiving payment for their export sale, regardless of the good intentions evidenced and fiscal responsibility exercised by their foreign buyers.

Don't-7: Don't confuse INCOTERMS with other sales terms formulations. Although all formulations of sales terms are similar, they are different in that each has its own definition of each individual term. Consequently, it is important to specify which sales terms formulation applies to your transaction. Additionally, it is important to insure that you don't misuse the specific INCOTERM selected and that you understand the costs, responsibilities, rights and obligations that accompany the use of a specific INCOTERM. The misuse of a selected INCOTERM can lead to over or underpayment of costs and to over or under assumption of responsibilities, rights and obligations.

Don't-8: Don't forget to analyse the adequacy of insurance coverage on your export transactions, given the transfer points for title and risk of loss and given the payment method selected. Determine the type and extent of insurance coverage required and assign responsibility for procurement and payment. Exporters that ignore these issues never comprehend the risk they've undertaken until the risk becomes actual and they discover that they are either uninsured or underinsured.

Don't-9: Don't think that your use of a letter of credit is a substitute for a valid, enforceable export sales contract. A letter of credit deals only with payment and the documents required to be presented to obtain payment. It does not deal with many other equally important issues, such as product acceptance, product warranties or dispute resolution procedures. These issues are typically dealt with in an export sales contract. An export sales contract should prescribe and incorporate the selected payment method and deal with any issue deemed significant to the exporter and the importer. Exporters who undertake an export transaction without having entered into an export sales contract are exposed to significant transaction risk over which they are unable to exercise much control.

Don't-10: Don't forget to insure consistency in your export transactions. By reviewing your selection of payment terms and sales terms against the terms of your export sales contract and the instruction letter given to your forwarder, you insure your transactions against problems that result from contradictory, overlapping information. Exporters that fail to perform a consistency check expose themselves to unnecessary errors that quickly and effortlessly unravel even the most soundly structured transaction.

Don't-11: Don't neglect to give a letter of instruction to your freight forwarder and to make sure that your freight forwarder carries errors and omission insurance. Exporters that fail to provide such instructions leave too much to fate and find themselves without recourse when fate works against them and they discover that their forwarder doesn't carry errors and omissions insurance and can't or won't make good on the problem.

Don't-12: Don't randomly assign your product a harmonised code number. Most countries in the world subscribe to the Harmonised Tariff Schedule to classify products for duty purposes. There is, however, often some room to manouver with regard to the applicable harmonised code for a particular product, i.e. there is generally not one absolutely correct product code. Since the choice of a harmonised code impacts the duty rate to be applied to a product and since duty rates vary country by country, it does not make sense to select one harmonised code over another, without also considering the applicable duty rates.

Don't -13: Don't ignore your responsibility to comply with the export laws as they relate to required export documents. Exporters are required to prepare and submit a Shippers Export Declaration (SED) for each export, unless an exemption applies. The SED must list the contents of each shipment, cite the appropriate export license, and identify the final destination, end user and end use. Failure to provide a SED exposes an exporter to civil and or criminal penalties.

Don't-14: Don't make any misrepresentations on your SED. Exporters are responsible for accurate SED's. Don't under-invoice or over-invoice your products on your SED to help an importing customer avoid tariffs or taxes. Don't misrepresent place of origin on your SED in order to assist your foreign buyer to gain access to a preferential duty programme to which your foreign buyer is not legitimately entitled.

These activities violate export laws and expose a exporter to civil and or criminal penalties. In addition, they expose the exporter to a potential violation of the importing country's tax law under the theory that the exporter aided and abetted the importer in committing tax fraud.

Don't -15: Don't neglect to comply with the record keeping requirements of export law. Exporters must maintain records of all exports for a period of 5 years. Exporters that fail to comply with the record keeping requirements of export law expose themselves to civil and or criminal penalties.

Don't -16: Don't forget to check out the applicability of two government sponsored cost savings programmes available to exporters, i.e Foreign Sales Corporations (FSC's) and duty drawback. FSC's offer exporters the opportunity to reduce federal income taxes on their export sales profits.

Don't-17: Don't be greedy — if an export opportunity looks too good to be true, it generally isn't true!

3

EXPORTING DIRECTLY AND INDIRECTLY

3.1. DIRECT EXPORTING

You can sell directly to customers in foreign markets by establishing an export department within your organisation. Selling through your company's sales department creates an opportunity to establish a closer relationship with the overseas market and buyer. In addition to selling directly to the market you wish to penetrate, you may also choose to use an export manager to handle other parts of the world.

In fact, in some countries, you cannot sell directly to the end-user, you must use a local agent or representative. This is true in the Middle East, Central America, and in some Asian countries. Other direct exporting options include using a variety of exportintermediaries.

3.1.1. Sales Agents

Generally, a agent or representative refers to a person who is responsible for closing the sale and taking orders on a commission basis. They do not take financial responsibility or collect payment for the goods sold, and they assume no risk or responsibility for the product. Remember that the primary interest of all salespeople is to make the sale, it is your responsibility to check credit and arrange payment terms. A representative will want a contract from you for:

1. Guaranteeing Territory.
2. Exclusivity.
3. Method of Compensation.
4. Term of Service.
5. Representation of the Product Line for a Definite Period of Time.

In most instances, the representative will be servicing both local and import accounts, as well as selling complimentary lines that do not compete. The representative utilises the product literature and samples that you supply. There is some controversy over the term agent. Depending on the country, the term carries a rather broad interpretation of legal responsibilities involving the agent's independent activity to contract on your behalf without your instruction. Avoid using the term agent. Any contract should clearly indicate legal authority of the representative to obligate the firm.

3.1.2. Foreign Distributor

The foreign distributor purchases the product and is always responsible for payment of the export item. They assume financial risk and generally provide support and service for the product. Distributors often buy to fill their own inventories and typically carry a range of non-competitive, but complementary products. Beware, some distributors have been known to take on products they purposely don't sell to check competition. The distributor should maintain adequate facilities and staff for day to day servicing. Investigate this option if your product requires maintenance or spare parts. Payment terms and length of contract time are usually initiated with a short trial period. Territory exclusivity is normally required by the distributor.

Selling directly to a foreign retailer relies mainly on traveling sales representatives. Another distribution alternative uses overseas buying offices of domestic retailers. These buyers can also be a practical source of foreign distribution for American manufacturers. Print based selling techniques that use catalogs, product literature, and brochures can also reach the marketing base of foreign retailers and they reduce the cost of traveling.

Product sales are usually limited to consumer goods which can be sold at a lower price, reflecting the absence of a representative's commission. It is recommended in Exporting From Start to Finance that you sell to the retailer at a price flexible enough to allow you to pay a representative in the future. In general, stores are more willing to select the service of a representative who places the order for them, and services their account with follow-up channels of communication.

3.1.3. Trading Companies

Buying offices or central trade offices are often divided into industry groups that buy for the whole country in some of the few remaining controlled market economies. China is the largest controlled economy that maintains trade and buying offices, often called Foreign Trade Corporations. They may buy for the whole country or for regional groups and provinces. Chinese trade organisations do most of the negotiating and contracting, which reduces the risk of bargaining with lower level officials who do not have ministry approval.

3.2. INDIRECT EXPORTING

While direct exporting may be a profitable method of foreign market entry for some businesses, sale by the exporter through an intermediary may be a better alternative to the complex tasks and risk involved in direct exporting.

An Export Management Company (EMC), functions as an "off-site" export sales department, representing your product along with various non-competitive manufacturers. The EMC searches for business for your company and usually provides the following services:

1. Performs market research and develops a marketing strategy.
2. Locates new and utilises existing foreign distributors or sales representatives to put your product into the foreign market.
3. Functions as an overseas distribution channel or wholesaler.
4. Takes title to the goods and operates on a commission basis.

Export Trading Companies (ETC) are very similar to Export Management Companies. The ETC is more likely to take title to the product and pay you directly, but like an EMC, they can also act as an export department. Usually, there is less responsibility on the part of the ETC towards the supplier and they tend to be demand driven and transaction oriented. There is legislation which promotes the use and formation of an EMC or ETC by providing the EMC/ETC with immunity from prosecution from antitrust regulations.

It permits banks to invest financially in EMCs/ETCs and reduces restrictions on trade financed by financial institutions. In contrast to an EMC, an ETC is very difficult to set up. There are special certifications and requirements, along with detailed paperwork. An example of an ETC is Mitsui; they buy and sell goods on their own behalf for their clients. Before deciding to use an EMC or ETC, consider these pros and cons.

3.2.1. Use of EMCs/ETCs

There are advantages and disadvantages to using an EMC or an ETC.

3.2.1.1. Advantages

1. Faster entry into the overseas market in terms of first recorded sales.
2. Better focus on exporting, because most firms give priority to their domestic problems.
3. Lower out-of-pocket expenses.
4. An opportunity to study the methods and potential of exporting.
5. Expertise in dealing with the special details involved in exporting, as well as its strategies.

3.2.1.2.Disadvantages

1. Loss of control of the export strategies and quality control of after-sales service.
2. Competition from the EMCs/ETCs other products.
3. Reluctance on the part of some foreign buyers to deal with a third party intermediary.
4. Some added costs, and higher selling prices because of gross profit margin requirements of the EMC/ ETC, unless the economies of scale can be used to off-set this factor.

5. The possibility of the EMC/ETC neglecting the client's product in favor of other products that might be more profitable and easier to sell.

3.2.2. Licensing

Licensing offers a small business the advantages of rapid entry into foreign markets as well as reducing the capital requirements to establish manufacturing facilities overseas.

Important considerations:

1. Be careful to protect trademarks and intellectual property by securing proper patent and trademark registration before signing a licensing contract.
2. Make sure agreements are not in violation of the host country's existing trade/product regulations or restrictions.
3. Don't wind up a competitor to your own product by having your own design or know-how used to compete in territories which you are selling directly.

Although the major disadvantage of licensing is the possibility of losing control over manufacturing and marketing, many times you can learn much more from your licensees by giving attention to original product improvements.

3.2.3. Franchising

Most companies already have successful domestic operations, with the most popular franchises occurring within the restaurant and retail sectors. Franchise agreements tend to give the franchiser more control over marketing, since it is the company's reputation and existing market relationship that adds value to the product. With almost any overseas arrangement, distribution approaches must incur expenses to support foreign marketing such as advertising. However, the overall investment by franchisers is much less than for company-owned sales outlets.

Companies like McDonalds and Coca Cola are prime examples of success in overseas markets. Japan, Europe, Australia and Asia are increasing their franchise development. Canada is also a high-ranking country for goods sold through franchise outlets, largely due to its location. The United Kingdom claims over 2500 franchise operations.

3.2.4. Agreements

Agreements with foreign manufacturers to produce your product, as opposed to exporting to the overseas region, are referred to as contract manufacturing. It is an easy foreign market entry method when your manufacturer is already producing your product for the domestic market. It can also be the initial instrument used to create a subsidiary company in a foreign country. Although it is a method of indirect distribution to foreign markets, it does not address sales and marketing issues of the finished product. These issues are;

1. How much intellectual knowledge should you deliver to the manufacturing firm to make contracting possible.
2. Quality control at overseas production facilities.
3. Lack of control over geographical, cultural or economic conditions.
4. Third party disclosure of confidential product information.

In contrast to licensing, contract manufacturing does accommodate company management roles in the foreign operation. However, you will also have to interact with entirely new management, located in a different country, whose first language is probably not English. Regardless of these disadvantages, the contracting manufacturer will have knowledge of the foreign market as well as the business and political contacts to facilitate market entry.

3.2.5. Other Intermediaries

3.2.5.1. Piggyback marketing

A company which already has an export distribution arrangement established may need to provide other goods or services to supplement the product. Permitting another company to market your product or service along with its own is called "piggyback" exporting. This type of exporting works well with accessory type products (computer hardware/software) or follow-up services where a third party adds value to the distribution system by offering a more complete solution to the foreign market.

3.2.5.2. Export merchants

These remarketers purchase and then re-package products (usually under their own label) to establish exclusive markets and customers. The main disadvantage of using export merchants is that your company could lose control over product pricing and marketing in overseas markets. Care should be taken to track the territories the remarketer's products are reaching to avoid interference with current export activities.

3.2.5.3. Corporate presence

Entering the foreign market by establishing an overseas presence requires careful planning and legal guidance.

Corporate presence decisions that involve the establishment of a foreign subsidiary as the primary method of selling to an international market are on the rise for both small and large companies. However there are alternative approaches to foreign distribution.

3.2.6. Joint Venture

Joint ventures bring together a foreign company and an American company with similar goals to establish a market entry and a distribution network. Each partner brings specialised skills that make significant contributions to manufacturing and distribution capabilities. Unique features of joint ventures include:

1. Joint ventures can be equity or non-equity partnerships.
2. In some countries, a joint venture is the only way an American company can set up operations.
3. Host country laws often require a citizen from that country to have a percentage of ownership.
4. Both partners make substantial investments into the venture.

Unlike licensing, joint ventures require a direct investment for management, technology transfer, training, and foreign relations. However, in a joint venture agreement, your company is in a position to expand resources, export experience and market knowledge while spreading the risk and laying a distribution framework. There are also several forms of tax advantages or waivers offered by foreign countries for joint ventures.

3.2.7. Strategic Alliances

Strategic Alliances is a broad term used to refer to

alternative alliances, other than joint ventures or subsidiaries. An alliance is a form of presence in the overseas market that represents more than a simple buy/sell agreement. It has a well structured purpose, shared management strategies and financial goal. Companies that form strategic alliances do not necessarily create an independent business organisation. For example, a strategic alliance may take the shape of any one, or combination of the following agreements:

1. Intellectual/Technology Sharing.
2. Cross-Licensing.
3. Distribution Arrangements.
4. Equity.
5. Product Development Coordination.

Many small businesses view strategic alliances as an alternative to capital intensive investment approaches to foreign market entry.

3.2.8. Subsidiaries

In contrast to a joint venture agreement, a subsidiary agreement guarantees control over all decisions involving marketing and production. Its technologies, patents, trademarks, and know-how have the maximum protection available under the host country's laws. A subsidiary is treated the same as host company operations in terms of benefits, regulations and taxes. For obvious reasons, there are choice places in the world to consider for jointly or wholly owned subsidiaries and manufacturing facilities.

Factors to consider range from low labour costs and government regulation to tax and economic incentives. Expert legal advice is recommended to determine true advantages of the subsidiary agreement within the laws and customs that are unique to the host country.

3.2.9. Finding Trade Leads

After deciding to pursue export methods for your product, you need to develop leads to opportunities with end users, distributors, and potential joint venture partners and representatives. If the buyer or end user is readily identified, this is simple. However, sometimes it is necessary to identify leads for the required buyers, distributors, representatives, or joint ventures. These are often available from a variety of government, public and private databases, programmes, and electronic resources.

Government agencies and sources are available from federal, state and local agencies. Private agencies and sources include chambers of commerce, business associations, trade shows, and traditional media sources. Electronic sources, including the Internet, represent the newest, fastest growing, and potentially most promising mechanism.

Many state and local governments will provide assistance to potential exporters although this will vary by locality and product. There is often a specific alliance between certain state and local governments and specific overseas counterparts such as "sister cities." Services often include:

1. *Trade Leads*: Usually available from agencies of state and local governments.
2. *Mission Planning Assistance and Introductions*: Frequently available at the state level in conjunction with trade shows arranged to showcase a variety of goods and services native to that state.
3. *Promotional Assistance*: Many state and even local governments realise the benefits to their economies by promoting exports for your organisation. Several fund print and electronic materials as well as hosting trade shows and supporting trade missions.

4. *Existing Contacts*: As with other government agencies, a database of previous contacts and interested parties are maintained by state and local government agencies from their prior activities.

3.2.10. Private Agencies

Existing business relationships and associations provide another avenue to making export connections and obtaining leads. These include:

— *Banks and other Financial Institutions*: Most larger banks and financial institutions are now multinational, have correspondent relationships with overseas counterparts, or maintain a department to handle foreign financial transactions. These can frequently provide leads and introductions to overseas markets.

— *Business Colleagues*: Business colleagues with existing relationships and firsthand experience may give personal recommendation or introductions to prospective representatives, buyers, or distributors.

— *Trade and Industry Associations*: Trade and industry associations are an excellent opportunity to share information and contacts with those having similar interests and contacts.

— *Trade Shows and Missions*: Trade shows and missions are one of the best ways to not only share information with other exporters, but provide the opportunity for direct contact with interested buyers, representatives, and distributors.

— *Export Seminars*: Seminars oriented towards exporting offer yet another opportunity to meet like-minded and experienced producers as well as developing additional expertise.

— *Chambers of Commerce*: Chambers of Commerce are normally involved in trade shows and missions. They maintain a database of contacts for those expressing interest in exports.

— *Miscellaneous Contacts*: Many times contacts can be made through unexpected sources such as freight carriers, shipping agents, airlines, commodities brokers, port authorities, and others can be a valuable source of information, contacts, and leads.

3.2.11. Electronic Informations

Traditionally, printed publications such as brochures and catalogs served to promote exports. However, the development of CD-ROMs, the Internet, and the availability of search and matching programmes on the Internet are resulting in an explosive increase in the use of electronic media.

Television and motion pictures can serve to elicit interest in several ways:

1. Primarily, direct advertising reaches a broad market quickly.
2. Secondly, the display of your product in a successful motion picture or television production can provide not only exposure, but also demand.
3. Finally, current methods of telecommunication permit the interactive review of products and their features with potential leads.

Electronic formats have the potential to accommodate all and replace many of the existing ways to locate leads. Electronic access to all previously listed government and private services, events, publications, and foreign associations is available.

4

PREPARING MY PRODUCT FOR EXPORT

Some exporters believe the domestic product can be exported without significant changes. Others seek to consciously develop uniform products that are acceptable in all markets. If the company manufactures more than one product or offers many models of a single product, it should start with the one best suited to the targeted market. Ideally, the firm chooses one or two products that fit the market without major design or engineering modifications. Doing so works best when the company:

1. Deals with international customers that have the same demographic characteristics or the same specifications for manufactured goods;
2. Supplies parts for goods that are exported to foreign countries without modifications;
3. Produces a unique product that is sold on the basis of its status or foreign appeal; or produces a product that has few or no distinguishing features and that is sold almost exclusively on a commodity or price basis.

4.1. PRODUCT ADAPTATION

To enter a foreign market successfully, a company may have to modify its product to conform to government regulations, geographic and climatic conditions, buyer preferences, or standards of living. The company may also need to modify its product to facilitate shipment or to compensate for possible differences in engineering and design standards. Foreign government product regulations are common in international trade and are expected to expand in the future. These regulations can take the form of high tariffs or nontariff barriers, such as regulations or product specifications. Governments impose these regulations to:

1. Protect domestic industries from foreign competition;
2. Protect the health of their citizens;
3. Force importers to comply with environmental controls;
4. Ensure that importers meet local requirements for electrical or measurement systems;
5. Restrict the flow of goods originating in or having components from certain countries; and
6. Protect their citizens from cultural influences deemed inappropriate.

It is often necessary for a company to adapt its product to account for geographic and climatic conditions as well as for the availability of resources. Factors such as topography, humidity, and energy costs can affect the performance of a product or even define its use. For example, the cost of petroleum products and the state of a country's infrastructure, may indicate the demand for energy-consuming products. Buyer preferences in a foreign market may also lead a manufacturer to modify its product.

Local customs, such as religious practices or the use of leisure time, often determine whether a product is marketable. The sensory impact of a product, such as taste or visual impact, may also be a critical factor. For example, Japanese tend to desire beautiful packaging. This has led many companies to redesign cartons and packages that are destined for this market. A country's standard of living can also determine whether a company needs to modify a product.

The level of income, education, and the availability of energy are all factors that help predict the acceptance of a product in a foreign market. If a less developed country, its market may be geared towards less sophisticated products. Certain high-technology products may not be successful in some countries not only because of their cost, but also because of their nature. For example, a computerised industrial washing machine that might replace workers could conflict with a country's employment goals.

Market potential must be large enough to justify the direct and indirect costs involved in product adaptation. The firm should assess the costs to be incurred and though it may be difficult, determine the increased revenues expected from adaptation. The decision to adapt a product is based partly on the degree of commitment to the specific foreign market; a firm with short-term goals will probably have a different perspective than a firm with long-term goals.

In addition to adaptations related to cultural and consumer preference, the exporter should be aware that even fundamental aspects of its products may require changing. For example, electrical standards in many foreign countries differ from electrical standards. It is not unusual to find phases, cycles, or voltages (for both residential and commercial use) that would damage or impair the operating efficiency of equipment designed for use in one's own country. These electrical standards sometimes vary even in the same country.

Knowing this requirement, the manufacturer can determine whether a special motor must be substituted or arrange for a different drive ratio to achieve the desired operating revolutions per minute. Similarly, many kinds of equipment must be engineered in the metric system for integration with other pieces of equipment or for compliance with the standards of a given country.

4.2. BRANDING AND LABELLING PRODUCTS

Consumers are concerned with both the product itself and the product's supplementary features, such as packaging, warranties, and service. Branding and labelling products in foreign markets raise new considerations for the company such as:

1. Are international brand names important to promote and distinguish a product? Conversely, should local brands or private labels be employed to heighten local interest?
2. Are the colours used on labels and packages offensive or attractive to the foreign buyer? For example, in some countries certain colours are associated with death.
3. Can labels be produced in official or customary languages if required by law or practice?
4. Does information on product content and country of origin have to be provided?
5. Are weights and measures stated in the local unit?
6. Must each item be labeled individually?
7. Are local tastes and knowledge considered? A dry cereal box picturing a athlete may not be as attractive to overseas consumers as the picture of a local sports hero.

A company may find that building international recognition for a brand is expensive. Protection for brand names varies from one country to another. In some developing countries, barriers to the use of foreign brands or trademarks may exist. In other countries, piracy of a company's brand names and counterfeiting of its products are widespread. To protect its products and brand names, a company must comply with local laws on patents, copyrights, and trademarks.

A firm may find it useful to obtain the advice of local lawyers and consultants when appropriate. The company may also find it advantageous to apply for a patent for its product, as well as applying for an international patent for the countries where it will be conducting business.

4.3. INSTALLATION OF PRODUCTS

Another element of product preparation that a company should consider is the ease of installing that product overseas. If technicians or engineers are needed overseas to assist in installation, the company should minimize their time in the field if possible. To do so, the company may wish to preassemble or pretest the product before shipping. Disassembling the product for shipment and reassembling abroad may be considered by the company. This method can save the firm shipping costs, but it may add to delay in payment if the sale is contingent on an assembled product.

The company should be careful to provide all product information, such as training manuals, installation instructions, and parts lists - all in the local language - even relatively simple instructions.

4.4. WARRANTIES ON THE PRODUCT

The company should include a warranty on the product

(and be very specific as to the warranty's coverage) since the buyer expects a specific level of performance and a guarantee that it will be achieved. Levels of expectation for a warranty vary by country depending upon its level of development, competitive practices, the activism of consumer groups, local standards of production quality, and other factors. A company may use warranties for advertising purposes to distinguish its product from the competition.

Strong warranties may be required to break into a new market, especially if the company is an unknown supplier. In some cases, warranties may be instrumental in making the sale and become a major element in negotiations. By providing an unnecessary warranty, the company may raise the cost of the product higher than the competitors' costs. When considering this point, exporters should keep in mind that servicing warranties will probably be more expensive and troublesome in foreign markets. It is desirable to arrange warranty service locally with the assistance of a representative or distributor.

4.5. PROMOTING THE PRODUCT

Advertising is necessary to sell your product. The advertising effort actually begins at home, as you make your first contacts with potential overseas representatives and introduce your company and product to target markets. In these early stages, you are beginning to establish your image This image is further refined by your negotiation and selection of your designated representative. Your conduct during negotiations and during foreign travel, even your choice of hotels, will characterise the image you are presenting.

There are two major considerations that must be addressed early in your selection of an advertising programme. First, you must decide who will control the advertising campaign, you or your overseas representative. Second, you must evaluate and implement the most appropriate methods. Frequently, there will be no "black and white" result from your evaluations. The promotional effort is often a collaboration between the exporter, his representative, and an advertising agency. A variety of advertising methods may be utilised to reach different aspects of the selected market.

The promotional campaign can be either centralised (under direct control of the exporter) or decentralised (under the control of the overseas representatives). Each method has its advantages and disadvantages. Centralised promotional efforts:

1. Control of all promotional efforts, logos, advertising messages by the exporter.
2. Uniformity of the company image and advertising message to all markets.
3. Economies of scale in maintaining one headquarters operation, minimising duplication of efforts.

Decentralised promotional efforts:

1. Each market is different and local experts may have the best understanding of it and the best methods to promote the product.
2. Ad agencies may not be strong or experienced in some overseas markets.
3. There is more flexibility in the selection of local advertising agencies.
4. Local regulations, customs, and taboos are more clearly understood.

As a beginning exporter, you will probably use the decentralised approach because you will be starting in one or a limited number of markets and require local expertise. As your markets expand or become more numerous, a more centralised approach with greater control and potential cost savings will become feasible. US advertising agencies can often affiliate with local firms to assure knowledge of the local market and effectiveness of the promotional effort.

No matter which means you select, close collaboration with your representative and constant communication is essential not only in determining the focus of your marketing effort, but also in monitoring and evaluating it. Once you determine who has control over the advertising campaign, you'll need to decide on the appropriate means to promote your product.

4.5.1. Methods for Marketing

A variety of methods and agencies are available to assist in your marketing effort, many of which you may be using in you domestic efforts. However, there are a number of methods that will help you advertise internationally. Some may be best utilised in a general sense, while other may be focused and specific to selected target markets. The following list represents the major methods:

4.5.1.1. Direct mail

The most time-tested and common method of advertising for smaller exporters is through a direct mail campaign. You may even be conducting your direct mail campaign ahead of, or as part of your effort to locate an overseas representative. Leads for direct mail can come from foreign trade and technical journals, trade association publications, responses to advertisements, or subscriber lists. Subscriber lists are often available from the publications, list brokers, or from direct mail consultants.

4.5.1.2. Media advertising

Media advertising is broader in scope than other methods. Television, video, and radio are general in their scope but well adapted for consumer products. A more specific approach, particularly for commercial products, is available through print media oriented towards specific markets. Whenever media advertising is used, make an effort to have it translated effectively in the local language, if possible. Screen it for conformance with the foreign country's customs, regulations, and note taboos or idiosyncrasies. There are several levels of international events and organised trips. These are frequently organised by state and government agencies, as well as trade associations. Some of the more prominent programmes are:

1. *Industry-organised Domestic Fairs and Exhibitions*: Most major industries in this country have their own organisation, many of which arrange regular exhibits of their member's products and services. Many attract potential buyers from around the world.
2. *Trade Shows and Trade Missions*: Organised trade associations, trade shows are an excellent opportunity to showcase your company and products as well as make valuable contacts.
3. *Matchmaker Events*: Often oriented to new-to-export firms, matchmaker events attempt to more closely align the exporter to prospective contacts and markets.
4. *Catalog Exhibitions*: Catalog and Video/Catalog exhibitions are a relatively low cost method to advertise your product abroad.

Careful planning and follow through are necessary when using methods requiring overseas travel due to the expense. The right event must be selected, materials and translators prepared and adequate follow-up assured.

4.6. SERVICING

Of special concern to foreign consumers is the service the company provides for its product. Service after the sale is critical for some products. Generally, the more complex the product's technology, the greater the demand for pre-sale and post-sale service. Therefore, there is pressure in some firms to offer simpler, more robust products overseas thereby reducing the need for maintenance and repairs. Suppliers who rely on foreign distributors or agents to provide service backup must take steps to ensure an adequate level of service. These steps include training, periodically checking service quality, and monitoring inventories of spare parts.

4.7. EXPORTING OF SERVICES

In global trade, many of the industries maintains a strong competitive lead are accompanied by sophisticated sales support. The following sectors have grown most rapidly from technology development and have particularly high export potential:

1. *Travel and tourism*: The largest single category within the service sector involves, quite simply, all businesses involved in its related services. Recreational and cultural services are also included. The industry is diverse and includes services in transportation, lodging, food and beverage service, recreation, purchase of incidentals consumed while in transit, and traveling on commercial airlines.
2. *Transportation services*: This sector includes aviation, ocean shipping, inland waterways, railroads, trucking, pipelines, and intermodal services as well as ancillary and support services in ports, airports,

railyards, and truck terminals. It is the indispensable service for international trade in goods moving all manufactured, mining, and agriculture products to market as well as transporting business and leisure travelers around the world.

3. *Architectural, construction, and engineering*: The vast experience and technological leadership of construction industry, as well as special skills in operations, maintenance, and management, frequently give firms a competitive edge in international projects. Some firms with expertise in specialised fields, such as electric power utilities, also export related design, construction, and engineering services.
4. *Education and training services*: Management training, technical training, and English language training are areas where expertise remains unchallenged. The export market for this training is almost limitless, encompassing most industry sectors, both products and services.
5. *Banking, financial, and insurance services*: Financial institutions are very competitive internationally, particularly when offering account management, credit card operations, and collection management. Insurers offer valuable services ranging from underwriting and risk evaluation to insurance operations and management contracts in the international marketplace.
6. *Entertainment*: Filmed entertainment and recorded music have been very successful in appealing to foreign audiences. Film companies license and sell rights to exhibit film in movie theaters, on television, and on videocassette. Music has been successful in both English-speaking and non-English-speaking countries.

7. *Information services*: This sector includes companies which generate, process, and export electronic commerce activities such as e-mail, funds transfer and data interchange, as well as data processing and network services, electronic information services, and professional computer services. The United States leads the world in marketing new technologies and enjoys a competitive advantage in computer operations, data processing and transmission, online services, computer consulting, and systems integration.
8. *Professional business services*: This sector includes accounting, advertising, legal, and management consulting services. The international market for these services is expanding at a more rapid rate than the domestic market. Organisations and business enterprises all over the world look to firms, as leaders in these sectors, for advice and assistance.

Services can be crucial in stimulating product exports and are critical in maintaining such transactions. Many merchandise exports would not take place if they were not supported by service activities such as banking, insurance, and transportation. There are, however, many obvious differences between services and products. Some aspects that differentiate the exporting of services from products include intangibiliy and customer involvement.

Since services are less tangible than products, communicating a service offer is much more difficult than communicating a product offer. Also, services frequently must be tailored to the specific needs of the client. This adaptation often necessitates the client's direct participation and cooperation. The involvement of the client requires the service provider to possess interpersonal skills and cultural sensitivity. The intangibility of services makes financing somewhat more difficult, given that no form of collateral is involved, and financial institutions may be less willing to provide financial support.

However, there are many public and private institutions that provide financial assistance to credit-worthy service exporters. Trade organisations offer two important finance services under various terms and conditions that are extremely valuable financing tools. One is a guarantee programme that requires the participation of an approved lender, while another programme provides loans or grants to the exporter or a foreign government. Exporters who insure their accounts receivable against commercial credit and political risk loss are usually able to secure financing from commercial banks and other institutions at lower rates and on a more liberal basis than would otherwise be the case.

Since service exports may be delivered in support of product exports, a sensible approach for some beginning exporters is to follow the path of complementary product exports. For years, many large accounting and banking firms have exported by following their major international clients abroad and continuing to assist them in their international activities. Smaller service exporters who cooperate closely with manufacturing firms are operating internationally and aim to provide service support for these manufacturers abroad. Also, a services firm may seek affiliation with a foreign firm in which opportunities exist. An agent, representative, or joint venture relationship could prove beneficial to the services firm. An indigenous services firm already has a knowledge of the various aspects of marketing in that country; i.e., regulations, restrictions, as well as the primary players, e.g., potential clients, competitors, etc.

5

MANAGING AND MOTIVATING DISTRIBUTORS

Successfully managing your distributors is a top priority for profitable international trade. If your linkage to international commerce is through your distributor, he or she represents your company. When your distributor prospers, you prosper, if you provide quality products with profit potential. Motivating and managing your distributor should generate a two-way relationship. There are certain services and responsibilities you expect from your distributor and the distributor in turn expects certain services and responsibilities from you. Working together or "partnering" can be beneficial from both sides. Use the following managing and motivating themes to build a collaborative relationship.

1. Work with the distributor on a regular basis. Avoid surprises, review sales figures and inventory data on a regular basis.
2. Develop a marketing plan every year with your distributor. Jointly work on periodic reviews and revisions of the marketing plan.
3. Schedule international sales meetings when necessary for new product launching or other special events.

4. Ask for new product ideas from your distributor. Modify your product accordingly to stay competitive within the market.
5. Try to work out differences. Changing distributors can be costly and lead to the end of product representation in that market.
6. Be flexible, blend your management style with your distributor's when necessary.
7. Be honest and sincere when interacting with your distributor.

Methods of motivating and encouraging your sales staff require special consideration for your overseas distributor. Rewards, incentives and recognition may take many forms, but consistent periodic recognition is essential for a positive overseas sales environment. Depending on the nature of your foreign market, some methods of recognition might include:

1. Print based recognition in the form of a prestigious plaque or certificate, announcement in the company newsletter, or recognition in the annual report or company profile. Use first names and business titles in the recognition.
2. Trips could include vacations with spouse or family, a visit to the company headquarters, or to trade shows, conferences and/or sales meetings. Some distributors may respond well to travel awards like golf or skiing.
3. Bonuses might include a cash award for personal recognition or an annual increased based on performance.
4. Entertainment, inclusion of spouses, and gifts of value might be an appropriate recognition in some countries. Records kept regarding preferred entertainment, favoured restaurants or popular

sports are useful. Keep a record of gifts presented in the past to avoid future duplication.

Notes on proper protocol will serve as the basis of your personal recognition programme for your distributor. You must be very careful to set up rewards that are acceptable to the culture, customs and preferences of the foreign market your distributor represents. Sensitivity to the unique cultural attitudes towards a reward system will help build a sincere relationship of trust and friendship.

5.1. SALES CONFERENCES

Sales conferences are an excellent source of motivation. They serve to inform, recognise sales efforts, and create new energy and enthusiasm. Your distributor will want to learn market updates, current product information, competitive sales programmes, and new sales techniques. It also allows the distributor to meet with other sales staff or distributors of your product and exchange ideas and useful tips.

5.2. QUALITY PRODUCTS

If a product is defective after it is sold, the distributor incurs both a monetary cost and an opportunity cost. The inconvenience goes beyond the time involved to ameliorate return and replacement factors. Regardless of the fact that you will replace the product at no cost, handling defective parts can be very costly in foreign trade due to shipping and duty fees. Your quality products should be:

1. Trouble free and carry warranties.
2. Unique to the intended target market.
3. Modify when necessary and stay ahead of competitors within the target market.

4. Delivered with appropriate, quality packaging.
5. Use proper language, colours, symbols and designs that are suitable and inoffensive in your market.
6. Supplied with high quality advertising and sales promotion techniques. For example, catalogs, brochures, display cases, banners, window cards, illuminated signs and fliers can be provided in lieu of advertising dollars.
7. Accompanied by easy to understand user manuals, information or instructions.
8. Patent or trademark protected.
9. It is your responsibility to take legal action against counterfeit merchandise brought into the target market and ensure your product will not be illegally imitated.

5.3. EXCLUSIVITY

Your distributor will want exclusive rights to your product with full control over his or her geographic territory. However, you cannot guarantee that sales to third or fourth parties will not find their way into foreign markets. One way to counter the inability to guarantee absolute exclusivity is to offer lower, preferential prices. You can also make a commitment to work with the foreign distributor to resolve problems of interference from competitors while discussing exclusivity of your product in advance.

5.4. SALES, PRICES AND PROFIT POTENTIAL

A good distributor will have business expansion plans. Focus on the distributor's sales, not his purchases from you. Increasing sales and profit growth are essential to business expansion. Accurate sales records signal market trends and slumps that help you stay ahead of the rest of the competitors in the marketplace. Compare sales growth records to other market indicators such as inflation, GNP, and data on consumer purchases. Motivate your distributor with reasonable payment terms that include periodic requests for payment delays.

Temporary payment terms during an economic slump or natural disaster is an effective way to build good will and establish loyalty. Managing advertising and sales promotions is also a critical factor of basic planning and forecasting. With your assistance, your distributors should develop periodic marketing plans. A marketing plan is necessary from your distributor so you can properly plan for advertising, sales promotions, and seasonal buying patterns. You can help your distributor plan for special sales and new product introductions as well as competitive trade-in programmes.

Sales and profit potential are the responsibility of the distributor. It is his responsibility to know the unique characteristics of his territory and be able to sell your product profitably within the existing system and methods of his market. In return, the distributor expects you will offer him the lowest price possible because:

1. The best competitive advantage in the market place is the lowest price.
2. He will have to take on some of your normal selling costs.
3. Your product accumulates additional price increases as a direct result of overseas transportation, duty and distribution fees.
4. Price discounts can be based upon the annual sales volume by the distributor, a single, large purchase order, cash payments, or large contract/sales opportunities.

5.5. EFFECTIVE COMMUNICATIONS TECHNIQUES

Effective communication techniques can build strong overseas relationships. Two important communication factors to consider when managing and motivating your international distributor are:

1. Your personal relationship with the distributor. Establish a rapport with the top person of the distributorship. That person has the power to make major decisions and effect change.
2. The cultural differences between countries. This includes socially acceptable practices, work ethics, language, religion, business ethics, attitudes, and values. Successfully working in an environment with cultural differences requires patience and a willingness to understand different cultures.

Overseas travel is very important, in fact, the only way to fully understand your foreign target market and foreign distributor is to visit them regularly. Relying on electronic or written communication can negate the factual evidence provided by on-site visits, research and interviews. Every distributor expects you to visit their market, he or she may also expect your technical experts, developers, and managers to visit as well. Spend several days learning about the problems and opportunities in that particular market. Utilise direct sources of information, attend trade shows, visit with top management, and be sure to include some contact with the end customer.

Establish a communication plan that:

1. Keeps your distributor informed.
2. Provides periodic new information about your product, company or industry.
3. Follows the 24 or 48 hour rule of responding. Always get back to inquiries and complaints within two days.

4. Avoids miscommunication by providing frequent information regarding invoicing, commissions, competitive updates and market analysis.
5. Informs your distributor of primary sources of help and information for opportunities with specific products.

Frequent communication is essential between you and your foreign distributor. A vital component of communication is quick response. The worst action you can take in international trade is no action. Timely and accurate administration of correspondence is expected not only with you but also your co-workers and managers. It can be in the form of:

1. Personal visits.
2. Phone.
3. Facsimile machine (fax).
4. Mail.
5. Electronic communications (Internet via e-mail).
6. Telecommunications.

The most widely accepted language is English, however for most of your distributors English will be a second language. This makes effective communication a requirement to overcome language differences.

5.6. TRAINING

Training support and materials will be expected by your distributor for the operation and sales features of your product. These materials can take many forms. Pamphlets, fliers, manuals, videos, onsite training visits, and slide presentations can be especially useful. Sales force training should include product and application knowledge, sales skills, and basic market research elements that identify customer profiles and product competition. The same support expectations apply towards after-sales service and repair methods. Technical training to support after-sales service in the exporting country should include:

1. Troubleshooting.
2. Repair and Testing Procedures.
3. Repair and Complaint Reporting.
4. Warranty Programme.

5.7. AFTER-SALE SERVICE

When considering service options, there are three basic options for providing after-sales support:

1. Train and assist your distributor to provide service.
2. Train an independent agency to provide service.
3. Relocate your own staff to service the foreign market.

These after-sales service departments can be structured to be profitable depending on market factors. However, a fast and efficient service operation will reduce additional costs to the end user while keeping a competitive advantage in the foreign market. It is to your benefit to have a flexible and swift repair system. Plan for spare parts and replacement items which may cost your distributor in the form of additional freight and/or duty fees.

6

LICENSING AND JOINT VENTURES IN EXPORT/IMPORT BUSINESS

6.1. TECHNOLOGY LICENSING

Technology licensing is a contractual arrangement in which the licensor's patents, trademarks, service marks, copyrights, trade secrets, or other intellectual property may be sold or made available to a licensee for compensation that is negotiated in advance between the parties. This compensation, or royalties, may be a lump sum royalty, a running royalty, or a combination of both. Companies frequently license their technology to foreign companies that then use it to manufacture and sell products in a country or group of countries defined in the licensing agreement.

A technology licensing agreement usually enables a firm to enter a foreign market quickly, and poses fewer financial and legal risks than owning and operating a foreign manufacturing facility or participating in an overseas joint venture. Licensing also permits firms to overcome many of the tariff and nontariff barriers that frequently hamper the export of manufactured products. For these reasons, licensing can be a particularly attractive method of "exporting" for small companies or companies with little international trade experience, even though licensing is profitably employed by small and large firms alike.

Technology licensing can also be used to acquire foreign technology such as, cross-licensing agreements or grantback clauses awarding rights to improved technology developed by a licensee. Technology licensing is not limited to the manufacturing sector. Franchising is also an important form of technology licensing used by many service industries. In franchising, the franchisor (licensor) permits the franchisee (licensee) to employ its trademark or service mark in a contractually specified manner for the marketing of goods or services.

The franchisor usually continues to support the operation of the franchisee's business by providing advertising, accounting, training, and related services and in many instances also supplies products needed by the franchisee. As a form of "exporting," technology licensing has certain potential drawbacks. One negative aspect of licensing is that control over the technology is weakened because it has been transferred to an unaffiliated firm. Additionally, licensing usually produces fewer profits than exporting actual goods or services.

In certain developing countries, there also may be problems in adequately protecting the licensed technology from unauthorised use by third parties. In considering the licensing of technology, it is important to remember that foreign licensees may attempt to use the licensed technology to manufacture products in direct competition with the licensor or its other licensees. As in all overseas transactions, it is important to investigate not only the prospective licensee but the licensee's country as well. The government of the host country often must approve the licensing agreement before it goes into effect. Some governments prohibit royalty payments that exceed a certain rate or contractual provisions barring the licensee from exporting products manufactured using the licensed technology to third countries.

The prospective licensor must always take into account the host country's:

1. Foreign patent, trademark, and copyright laws;
2. Exchange controls;
3. Product liability laws;
4. Possible countertrading or barter requirements;
5. Antitrust and tax laws; and
6. Government attitudes toward repatriation of royalties and dividends.

In a few instances, international technology licensing agreements can unlawfully restrain trade in violation offoreign antitrust laws. As a general rule, antitrust laws prohibit international technology licensing agreements that unreasonably restrict imports of competing goods or technology or unreasonably restrain domestic competition or exports by persons. Whether or not a restraint is reasonable is a fact-specific determination that is made after consideration of the availability of:

1. Competing goods or technology;
2. Market shares;
3. Barriers to entry;
4. The business justifications for and the duration of contractual restraints; and,
5. Valid patents, trademarks, and copyrights.

Foreign countries have strict antitrust laws that affect technology licensing. Because of the potential complexity of international technology licensing agreements, firms should seek qualified legal advice before entering into such an agreement. In many instances, licensors should also retain qualified legal counsel in the host country in order to obtain advice on applicable local laws and to receive assistance in securing the foreign government's approval of the agreement. Sound legal advice and thorough investigation of the prospective licensee and the host country will increase the likelihood that your licensing agreement will be a profitable transaction.

6.2. JOINT VENTURES IN FOREIGN TRADE

In some cases, joint ventures provide the best partner-like manner of obtaining foreign trade income. The firm then choses to begin a business relationship with a firm in the host country. International joint ventures are used in a wide variety of manufacturing, mining, and service industries and frequently involve technology licensing by the firm to the joint venture. Host country laws may require that a certain percentage (often 51 percent or more) of manufacturing or mining operations be owned by nationals of that country, thereby limiting firms' local participation to minority shares of joint ventures.

In addition to such legal requirements, firms may find it desirable to enter into a joint venture with a foreign firm to help spread the high costs and risks frequently associated with foreign operations. The local partner will likely bring to the joint venture its knowledge of the customs and tastes of the people, an established distribution network, and valuable business and political contacts. Having a local partner may also lessen the "foreigner" image of the firm and thus may provide some protection against discrimination or expropriation if conditions change.

There are some possible disadvantages to international joint ventures. A major potential drawback of joint ventures, especially in countries that limit foreign companies to minority participation, is the loss of effective managerial control. This can result in reduced profits, increased operating costs, inferior product quality, exposure to product liability, and environmental litigation and fines. Firms that wish to retain effective managerial control will find this issue an important topic in negotiations with the prospective joint venture partner and the host government.

Like technology licensing agreements, joint ventures can raise anti-trust issues in certain circumstances, particularly when the prospective joint venture partners are major existing or potential competitors in the affected national markets. Firms may wish to consider applying for an export trade certificate of review from the department of commerce or a business review letter from the department of justice when significant anti-trust issues are raised by the proposed international joint venture.

Because of the complex legal issues frequently raised by international joint venture agreements, it is very important, to seek legal advice from qualified counsel before entering into any such agreement. Firms contemplating international joint ventures should consider retaining experienced counsel in the host country. Firms can find it very disadvantageous to rely upon their potential joint venture partners to negotiate host government approvals and advise them on legal issues, since their prospective partners' interests may not always coincide with their own. Qualified foreign counsel can be very helpful in obtaining government approvals and providing ongoing advice regarding the host country's intellectual property, tax, labour, corporate, commercial, antitrust, and exchange control laws.

7

PAYMENT METHODS IN EXPORTS AND IMPORTS BUSINESS

Importing and exporting can be complicated and expensive; there are many rules, regulations, and situations that need taking into account. Here is a look at some of the most important things to look at when you want to start importing and/or exporting. The most important thing to look at when you plan importing or exporting is whether the products you are moving are able to be imported. Each country will have a different list of restricted products. You should always find out as soon as possible if the product you wish to move is restricted.

A crucial element of importing or exporting is knowing that the product will work. When importing, do you need to add the cost of modifications or extras to the product price, and will your customers be happy paying for them, particularly if there are no English instructions; or will you be forced to cover their cost? When exporting, will the buyers be happy paying for the extras, or will they expect you to pay for them? Are they aware that the product may be unusable without them? Are they aware that the product may not have instructions in French?

7.1. PAYMENT METHODS

It is important to remember that when you import or export goods, you may be required to pay (or accept payment) in a number of currencies. You need to arrange with the supplier or buyer in advance who will bear the costs of exchanging the currency; this can affect the costs a considerable amount and may need some negotiation to find the fairest option. In most cases the buyer (importer) will pay the currency conversion charges, although it now a lot easier for payment to be converted as it enters the bank account.

7.1.1. Prudent Credit Practices

An experienced exporting firm extends credit cautiously. It evaluates new customers with care and continuously monitors older accounts. Such a firm may wisely decide to decline a customer's request for open account credit if the risk is too great and propose instead payment on delivery terms through a documentary sight draft or irrevocable confirmed letter of credit or even payment in advance. On the other hand, for a fully creditworthy customer, the experienced exporter may decide to allow a month or two to pay, perhaps even on open account.

Other good credit practices include being aware of any unfavourable changes in your customers' payment patterns, refraining from going beyond normal commercial terms, and consulting with your international banker n how to cope with unusual circumstances or in difficult markets. It is always advisable to check a buyer's credit (even if safest payment methods are employed). A Department of Commerce International Company Profile (ICP) provides useful information for credit checks. For a fee, an ICP may be requested on foreign companies in many countries.

It contains financial information on the company and a discussion regarding its size, capitalisation, years in business, and other information such as citing some U.S. companies that conduct business with the firm. The exporter can then contact the companies to find out about their payment experience with the foreign firm. ICPs are not available in every country, and in these instances, EACs can provide a list of private credit reporting services. There are several companies that compile financial information on foreign firms (particularly larger firms) and make it available to their subscribers.

Also, banks are sometimes able to provide credit reports on foreign companies, either through their own foreign branches or through a correspondent bank. As being paid in full and on time is of the utmost concern to exporters, the level of risk in extending credit is a major consideration. There are several ways in which you can receive payment when selling your products abroad, depending on how trustworthy you consider the buyer to be. Typically with domestic sales, if the buyer has good credit, sales are made on open account; if not, cash in advance is required. For export sales, these ways are not the only common methods. Listed in order from most secure for the exporter to the least secure, the basic methods of payment are:

1. Cash in advance;
2. Documentary letter of credit;
3. Documentary collection or draft;
4. Open account; and
5. Other payment mechanisms, such as consignment sales.

7.1.2. Cash in Advance

This is the most preferable method of payment for a small

business looking to export. It helps keep your cash flow positive, and minimises your risk in exporting. The main drawback is that few buyers will be willing to pay in advance, in case of problems with the order. One solution is to arrange for part payment in advance. This provides some security that you will be paid, and helps to fund the cost of production and shipping; whilst allowing the buyer to check the quality of the goods before parting with the rest of their money. Payment in advance is not preferable if you are importing, but if you are left with no other option, be certain to take Goods in Transit Insurance to help cover you against any problems.

Receiving payment by cash in advance of the shipment might seem ideal. In this situation, the exporter is relieved of collection problems and has immediate use of the money. A wire transfer is commonly used and has the advantage of being almost immediate. Payment by check, may result in a collection delay of up to six weeks. Therefore, this method may defeat the original intention of receiving payment before shipment. Many exporters accept credit cards in payment for exports of consumer and other products, generally of a low follar value, sold directly to the end user.

Domestic and international rules governing credit card transactions sometimes differ, so merchants should contact their credit card processor for more specific information. International credit card transactions are typically done by telephone or fax. Due to the nature of these methods, exporters should be aware of fraud. Merchants should determine the validity of transactions and obtain the proper authorisations. For the buyer, however, advance payment tends to create cash flow problems, as well as increase risks.

Furthermore, cash in advance is not as common in most of the world as it is in the United States. Buyers are often concerned that the goods may not be sent if payment is made in advance. Exporters that insist on this method of payment as their sole method of doing business may find themselves losing out to competitors who offer more flexible payment terms.

7.1.3. Documentary Collection

This where the exporter/seller sends a number of documents to the customer's bank; when the customer pays in full, the bank gives them the import and release documents (DP). In some cases, the customer will sign a 'bill of exchange', which sets out a specific number of days to pay. When the customer signs the bill, they will receive the import and release documents (DA).

This is an effective method of payment for small businesses, as it helps provide security for both the buyer and seller. You must be sure however, if allowing a number of days to pay, that the customer is reliable and creditworthy. Otherwise you may be left needing to claim in court to retrieve your money, which is especially difficult with foreign companies.

7.1.4. Documentary Letters and Drafts

Documentary letters of credit or documentary drafts are often used to protect the interests of both buyer and seller. These two methods require that payment be made based on the presentation of documents conveying the title and that specific steps have been taken. Letters of credit and drafts can be paid immediately or at a later date. Drafts that are paid upon presentation are called sight drafts. Drafts that are to be paid at a later date, often after the buyer receives the goods, are called time drafts or date drafts. Since payment by these two methods is made on the basis of documents, all terms of payment should be clearly specified in order to avoid confusion and delay.

Banks charge fees - based mainly on a percentage of the amount of payment - for handling letters of credit and smaller amounts for handling drafts. If fees charged by both the foreign and banks are to be applied to the buyer's account, this should be explicitly stated in all quotations and in the letter of credit. The exporter usually expects the buyer to pay the charges for the letter of credit, but some buyers may not agree to this added cost. In such cases, the exporter must either absorb the costs of the letter of credit or risk losing that potential sale. Letters of credit for smaller amounts can be somewhat expensive since fees can be high relative to the sale.

7.1.5. Letters of Credit

A letter of credit adds a bank's promise to pay the exporter to that of the foreign buyer provided that the exporter has complied with all the terms and conditions of the letter of credit. The foreign buyer applies for issuance of a letter of credit from the buyer's bank to the exporter's bank and therefore is called the applicant; the exporter is called the beneficiary. Payment under a documentary letter of credit is based on documents, not on the terms of sale or the physical condition of the goods.

The letter of credit specifies the documents that are required to be presented by the exporter, such as an ocean bill of lading (original and several copies), consular invoice, draft, and an insurance policy. The letter of credit also contains an expiration date. Before payment, the bank responsible for making payment, verifies that all document conform to the letter of credit requirements. If not, the discrepancy must be resolved before payment can be made and before the expiration date.

A letter of credit issued by a foreign bank is sometimes confirmed by a bank. This confirmation means that the bank (the confirming bank), adds its promise to pay to that of the foreign bank (the issuing bank). If a letters of credit is not confirmed, it is advised through a bank and thus called an advised letter of credit. Exporters may wish to confirm letters of credit issued by foreign banks if they are unfamiliar with the foreign banks or concerned about the political or economic risk associated with the country in which the bank is located.

A letter of credit may either be irrevocable and thus, unable to be changed unless both parties agree; or revocable where either party may unilaterally make changes. A revocable letter of credit is inadvisable as it carries many risks for the exporter. A change made to a letter of credit after it has been issued is called an amendment. Banks also charge fees for this service. It should be specified in the amendment if the exporter or the buyer will pay these charges. Every effort should be made to get the letter of credit right the first time since these changes can be time-consuming and expensive. To expedite the receipt of funds, wire transfers may be used. Exporters should consult with their international bankers about bank charges for such services.

7.1.5.1. Tips on Using a Letter of Credit

When preparing quotations for prospective customers, exporters should keep in mind that banks pay only the amount specified in the letter of credit - even if higher charges for shipping, insurance, or other factors are incurred and documented. Upon receiving a letter of credit, the exporter should carefully compare the letter's terms with the terms of the exporter's pro forma quotation. This step is extremely important, since the terms must be precisely met or the letter of credit may be invalid and the exporter may not be paid. If meeting the terms of the letter of credit is impossible or if any of the information is incorrect or even misspelled, the exporter should contact the customer immediately and ask for an amendment to the letter of credit.

The exporter must provide documentation showing that the goods were shipped by the date specified in the letter of credit or the exporter may not be paid. Exporters should check with their freight forwarders to make sure that no unusual conditions may arise that would delay shipment. Documents must be presented by the date specified for the letter of credit to be paid. Exporters should verify with their international bankers that there will be sufficient time to present the letter of credit for payment. Exporters may request that the letter of credit specify that partial shipments and transshipment will be allowed. Specifying what will be allowed can prevents unforeseen last minute problems.

7.1.6. Documentary Drafts

A draft, sometimes also called a bill of exchange, is analogous to a foreign buyer's check. Like checks used in domestic commerce, drafts carry the risk that they will be dishonored. However, in international commerce, title does not transfer to the buyer until he pays the draft, or at least engages a legal undertaking that the draft will be paid when due.

7.1.7. Sight Drafts

A sight draft is used when the exporter wishes to retain title to the shipment until it reaches its destination and payment is made. Before the shipment can be released to the buyer, the original ocean bill of lading (the document that evidences title) must be properly endorsed by the buyer and surrendered to the carrier. It is important to note that air waybills of lading, on the other hand, do not need to be presented in order for the buyer to claim the goods. Hence, risk increases when a sight draft is being used with an air shipment. In actual practice, the ocean bill of lading is endorsed by the exporter and sent via the exporter's bank to the buyer's bank.

It is accompanied by the sight draft, invoices, and other supporting documents that are specified by either the buyer or the buyer's country. The foreign bank notifies the buyer when it has received these documents. As soon as the draft is paid, the foreign bank turns over the bill of lading thereby enabling the buyer to obtain the shipment. There is still some risk when a sight draft is used to control transferring the title of a shipment.

The buyer's ability or willingness to pay might change from the time the goods are shipped until the time the drafts are presented for payment; there is no bank promise to pay standing behind the buyer's obligation. Additionally, the policies of the importing country could also change. If the buyer cannot or will not pay for and claim the goods, returning or disposing of the products becomes the problem of the exporter.

7.1.8. Time Drafts and Date Drafts

A time draft is used when the exporter extends credit to the buyer. The draft states that payment is due by a specific time after the buyer accepts the time draft and receives the goods. By signing and writing "accepted" on the draft, the buyer is formally obligated to pay within the stated time. When this is done the time draft is then called a trade acceptance. It can be kept by the exporter until maturity or sold to a bank at a discount for immediate payment. A date draft differs slightly from a time draft in that it specifies a date on which payment is due, rather than a time period after the draft is accepted.

When either a sight draft or time draft is used, a buyer can delay payment by delaying acceptance of the draft. A date draft can prevent this delay in payment though it still must be accepted. When a bank accepts a draft, it becomes an obligation of the bank and thus, a negotiable investment known as a banker's acceptance. A banker's acceptance can also be sold to a bank at a discount for immediate payment.

7.1.9. Open Account

An open account is where you credit check the buyer, and organise an appropriate credit limit and credit period for payment. When you ship the goods, the payment is due a set number of days after. This type of payment method is normally used only in strong or long-term business relationships, where you can be sure that the buyer will pay. This type of payment is preferable to small businesses when importing, helping you keep positive cash flow. It is however much more preferable to have payment in advance when exporting.

In a foreign transaction, an open account can be a convenient method of payment if the buyer is well established, has a long and favourable payment record, or has been thoroughly checked for creditworthiness. With an open account, the exporter simply bills the customer, who is expected to pay under agreed terms at a future date. Some of the largest firms abroad make purchases only on open account. However, there are risks to open account sales. The absence of documents and banking channels might make it difficult to pursue the legal enforcement of claims.

The exporter might also have to pursue collection abroad, which can be difficult and costly. Another problem is that receivables may be harder to finance, since drafts or other evidence of indebtedness are unavailable. There are several ways to reduce credit risk, through such means as export credit insurance and factoring. Exporters contemplating a sale on open account terms should thoroughly examine the political, economic, and commercial risks. They should also consult with their bankers if financing will be needed for the transaction before issuing a pro forma invoice to a buyer.

7.1.10. Consignment Sales

International consignment sales follow the same basic procedures as in the United States. The goods are shipped to a foreign distributor who sells them on behalf of the exporter. The exporter retains title to the goods until they are sold, at which point payment is sent to the exporter. The exporter has the greatest risk and least control over the goods with this method. Additionally, receiving payment may take quite a while. It is wise to consider risk insurance with international consignment sales. The contract should clarify who is responsible for property risk insurance that will cover the merchandise until it is sold and payment is received. In addition, it may be necessary to conduct a credit check on the foreign distributor.

7.1.11. Countertrade

International countertrade is a trade practice whereby one party accepts goods, services, or other instruments of trade in partial or whole payment for its products. This type of trade fulfills financial, marketing, or public policy objectives of the trading parties. There are several types of countertrade, including counterpurchase and barter. Counterpurchase is quite common. In this situation, exporters agree to purchase a quantity of goods from a country in exchange for that country's purchase of the exporter's product. These goods are typically unrelated but have an equivalent value. Another form of this practice is contractually linked, parallel trade transactions that each involve a separate financial settlement.

Barter arrangements in international commerce are not as common, because the parties' needs for the goods of the other seldom coincide and because valuation of the goods may be problematic. This type of countertrade occurs without money exchanging hands as merchandise is traded directly for other merchandise or services. Barter might occur by swapping (one good for another) or by switching (using a chain of buyers and sellers in different markets to barter). Exporters can take advantage of countertrade opportunities by trading through an intermediary with countertrade expertise, such as an international broker, an international bank, or an export management company.

One drawback to this type of exporting is that there are often higher transaction costs and greater risks than with other kinds of export transactions.

7.1.12. Foreign Currency

A buyer and a seller who are in different countries rarely use the same currency. Payment is usually made in either the buyer's or the seller's currency or in a third mutually agreed-upon currency. One of the risks associated with foreign trade is the uncertainty of the future exchange rates. The relative value between the two currencies could change between the time the deal is concluded and the time payment is received. If the exporter is not properly protected, a devaluation or depreciation of the foreign currency could cause the exporter to lose money.

If the buyer asks to make payment in a foreign currency, the exporter should consult an international banker before negotiating the sales contract. Banks can offer advice on the foreign exchange risks that exist with a particular currency. Some international banks can also help hedge against such a risk, by agreeing to purchase the foreign currency at a fixed price in dollars, regardless of the currencies value at the time the customer pays. Banks will normally charge a fee or discount the transaction for this service. If this mechanism is used, the bank's fee should be included in the price quotation.

7.1.13. Delivery Terms

It is essential that all importing or exporting be covered by an effective set of delivery terms. In the event of a late or damaged delivery, the costs to the importer could be huge. Incoterms are a set of international standard definitions that allow terms to be set without the risk of confusion, even when translated into different languages. Incoterms help to set out fair compensation rules in the event of a late, damaged, or missing delivery. They can also set out fair payment details once a complete delivery has been made.

7.1.14. Insurance

One way to protect your business against a damaged or late delivery is to take out Goods in Transit Insurance. This covers the goods against damage, loss, late delivery or no delivery while in transit, providing cover against the damage that a late delivery can cause to a buyer. This is particularly important if you are an exporter, as the cost of replacing goods will usually be very high, as well as the cost of the business you may lose because of the problem.

7.2. PROBLEMS IN PAYMENT SYSTEM

In international trade, problems involving bad debts are more easily avoided than rectified after they occur. Nonetheless, just as in a company's domestic business, exporters occasionally encounter problems with buyers who default on their payment. When these problems occur in international trade, obtaining payment can be both difficult and expensive. Even when the exporter has insurance to cover commercial credit risks, a default by a buyer still requires the time, effort, and cost of the exporter to collect a payment.

The exporter must exercise normal business prudence in exporting and exhaust all reasonable means of obtaining payment before an insurance claim is honored. Even then there is often a significant delay before the insurance payment is made. The simplest solution to a payment problem is to contact and negotiate with the customer. With patience, understanding, and flexibility, an exporter can often resolve conflicts to the satisfaction of both sides. This point is especially true when a simple misunderstanding or technical problem is to blame and there is no question of bad faith. Even though the exporter may be required to compromise on certain points - perhaps even on the price of the committed goods - the company may save a valuable customer and profit in the long run.

However, if negotiations fail and the sum involved is large enough to warrant the effort, a company should obtain the assistance and advice of its bank, legal counsel, and other qualified experts. Since arbitration is often faster and less costly, this step is preferable to legal action if both parties can agree to take their dispute to an arbitration agency. The International Chamber of Commerce handles the majority of international arbitration and is usually acceptable to foreign companies because it is not affiliated with any single country.

7.3. REGULATIONS AND TAXES

It is vital to ensure that you pay the correct duties and

VAT on all products that you import. There are number of different excise duties that apply to goods, and you need to be sure that you are paying the correct rates. In the majority of cases, you do not need to charge duty or VAT on exports. You must have official or commercial evidence of non-EU exports to not charge VAT. The rules are different depending on the product and whether it is being exported in or out of the EU. Before you start exporting, you must make sure that you are fully aware of any duty or VAT you need to pay when exporting.

As small businesses may not be VAT registered, the rules will vary depending on the product, you should be certain to clarify the duty or VAT you will need to pay, and how this will change if you register for VAT in the near future. Depending on the amount you import and export, some business will be entitled to claim back some of the duty or VAT payments that you make. A number of businesses are also entitled to delay payment of duties.

If you are importing from outside of the EU or from special EU territories, then the goods you bring in will almost always need to be entered and declared to Customs and Excise as they arrive. The vast majority of exports outside of the EU or to special EU territories also need to be declared to Customs and Excise as they leave the country. If you are importing or exporting from within the EU, then a customs declaration is not usually necessary. Although if you are VAT registered, and your EU imports or exports exceed a set amount you will need to fill in a supplementary declaration form each month.

7.4. IMPORT/EXPORT TRAINING

The exact details of import and export regulations are long and complicated, one way to help improve your businesses ability is to undertake import/export training.

This will help you (or a chosen employee) to understand in more detail the rules and regulations regarding the products you move. This will help to ensure that you pay all necessary duty, and are able to claim back all the money you may be entitled to. The cost of training can be quite high, but if your business is looking at importing or exporting in the long term, then the cost will usually be more than worth it.

8

FINANCING EXPORT TRANSACTION

Exporters naturally want to get paid as quickly as possible, while importers usually prefer to delay payment until they have received or resold the goods. Because of the intense competition for export markets, being able to offer attractive payment terms customary in the trade is often necessary to make a sale. Exporters should be aware of the many financing options open to them so that they choose the most acceptable one to both the buyer and the seller. In many cases, government assistance in export financing for small and medium-sized businesses can increase a firm's options.

8.1. FINANCIAL DECISION-MAKING

The following factors are important to consider in making decisions about financing:

1. *The need for financing to make the sale*: In some cases, favorable payment terms make a product more competitive. If the competition offers better terms and has a similar product, a sale can be lost. In other cases, the buyer may have preference for buying from a particular exporter, but might buy your product because of shorter or more secure credit terms.

2. *The length of time the product is being financed*: This determines how long the exporter will have to wait before payment is received and influences the choice of how the transaction is financed.
3. *The cost of different methods of financing*: Interest rates and fees vary. Where an exporter can expect to assume some or all of the financing costs, their effect on price and profit should be well understood before a pro forma invoice is submitted to the buyer.
4. *The risks associated with financing the transaction*: The riskier the transaction, the harder and more costly it will be to finance. The political and economic stability of the buyer's country can also be an issue. To provide financing for either accounts receivable or the production or purchase of the product for sale, the lender may require the most secure methods of payment, a letter of credit (possibly confirmed), or export credit insurance or guarantee.
5. *The need for pre-shipment finance and for post-shipment working capital*: Production for an unusually large order, or for a surge of orders, may present unexpected and severe strains on the exporter's working capital. Even during normal periods, inadequate working capital may curb an exporter's growth.

8.2. FOREIGN BUYERS

Foreign buyers often press exporters for longer payment periods. While it is true that liberal financing is a means of enhancing export competitiveness, exporters need to weigh carefully the credit or financing they extend to foreign customers. Moreover, the extension of credit by the seller to the buyer is more common. Sellers who are reluctant to extend credit may face the possibility of the loss of the sale to their competitors. A useful guide for determining the appropriate credit period is the normal commercial terms in the exporter's industry for internationally traded products.

Buyers generally expect to receive the benefits of such terms. For off-the-shelf items like consumer goods, chemicals, and other raw materials, agricultural commodities, and spare parts and components, normal commercial terms range with few exceptions from 30 to 180 days. Custom-made or high-value capital equipment, on the other hand, may warrant longer repayment periods. Once credit terms are extended to a buyer, they tend to be precedent for future sales, so the exporter should review with special care any credit terms extended to first-time buyers. Exporters should follow the same careful credit principals they follow for domestic customers.

An important reason for controlling the credit period is the cost incurred through use of working capital or through interest and fees. If the buyer is not responsible for paying these costs, then the exporter should factor them into the selling price. The exporter also should recognise that longer credit periods may increase any risk of default. Thus, the exporter must exercise judgement in balancing competitiveness against consideration of cost and safety. Customers are frequently charged interest on credit periods of a year or longer but less frequently on short-term credit.

Most exporters absorb interest charges for short-term credit unless the customer pays after the due date. Obtaining cash immediately is usually a high priority with exporters. Converting export receivables to cash at a discount with a bank is one way to do so. Another way is to expand working capital resources. A third approach, suitable when the purchase involves capital goods and the repayment period extends a year or longer, is to arrange for third-party financing. An example of this is a bank making a loan directly to the buyer for the product, with the exporter being paid immediately from the loan proceeds while the bank waits for payment and earns interest. A fourth possibility, when financing is difficult to obtain, is to engage in countertrade to afford the customer an opportunity to generate earnings with which to pay for the purchase.

These options may involve the payment of interest, fees, or other costs by the exporter. Some options are more feasible when the amounts are in larger denominations. Exporters should also determine whether they incur financial liability should the buyer default.

8.3. COMMERCIAL BANKING FACILITIES

The same commercial bank facilities used to finance domestic activities, including revolving lines of credit for working capital, are often sought to finance export sales until payment is received. Banks do not regularly extend financing solely on the basis of an individual order as they prefer to establish an ongoing business relationship. A logical first step for an exporter seeking to finance short-term export sales is to approach the local commercial bank with which it already does business. If the bank previously has extended credit to the exporter, the bank will be familiar with the exporter's financial standing, credit need, repayment record, and ability to perform.

The bank may be willing to raise the overall limit on an existing working capital line of credit, expand its scope to cover export transactions, or approve a separate line specifically adapted to export-related transactions such as discounting. Alternatively, the exporter may wish to approach a commercial bank with an international department. Such a bank will be familiar with export business and also be in a position to provide international banking services related to documentary collections and letters of credit, including the discounting of drafts. An intermediate approach is to retain a relationship with the exporter's bank, but seek a referral to a correspondent bank that has an international department.

The exporter should visit the bank's international department, to discuss export plans, available banking facilities, and applicable charges. The exporter may wish to inquire about such matters as: fees for amending or confirming a letter of credit; processing drafts; and about the bank's experience in working with Government agencies that offer export financing assistance. Generally, the bank's representative handing the exporter's account will not be lodged in the international department. It is in the exporter's best interest to create and foster a close working relationship with the international department.

The responsibility for repaying a working capital loan ordinarily rests with the exporter, even if the foreign buyer fails to pay. The bank takes this contingency into account in deciding on an export working capital line of credit. It is to the benefit of the bank and the exporter to improve the quality of the export receivables by using letters of credit, by making use of credit insurance, or by using export-import bank or small business administration working capital guarantees. An exporter shipping capital goods may want the commercial bank to make medium-term loans directly to the foreign buyer to finance the sale.

Such loans are available for well-established foreign buyers in more stable markets, but where there is an element of risk, the bank may require a standby letter of credit, recourse on the exporter in case of default, or similar repayment reinforcement. The exporter should be knowledgeable about loans from his own bank with Export-Import Bank medium- and long-term export guarantee programmes, assuming that the commercial bank is willing to utilise them.

A time draft under an irrevocable letter of credit confirmed by a bank presents relatively little risk of default, so an exporter may be willing to hold such a draft until it matures. Unless the exporter has ample funds needed for other purposes, holding drafts will use up working capital. As another course of action, the exporter's bank may be willing to buy, or lend against, time drafts from an exporter that a creditworthy foreign buyer has accepted or agreed to pay at a specified future date. This in effect converts the time draft into immediate cash.

The amount received by the exporter is less than the face value of the draft. The difference, called a "discount," represents interest and fees that the bank charges for holding the draft until maturity. The bank may also require the exporter to reimburse the bank in case the draft is unpaid at the due date. In a third instance, a commercial bank may undertake to accept the obligation of paying a draft for a fee; this is called a banker's acceptance. Banker's acceptances are usually in large denominations. Only a few well-known banks are accepted in the market as "prime-name" banks for purposes of creating banker's acceptances.

8.3.1. Factoring, Forfaiting, and Confirming

Factoring is the discounting of a foreign account receivable that does not involve a draft. The exporter transfers title to its foreign accounts receivable to a factoring house (an organisation that specialises in the financing of accounts receivable) for cash at a discount from the face value. Although factoring is sometimes done without recourse to the exporter, the specific arrangements should be verified by the exporter. Factoring of foreign accounts receivable is less common than factoring of domestic receivables.

Forfaiting is the selling, at a discount, of longer term accounts receivable or promissory notes of the foreign buyer. These instruments may also carry the guarantee of the foreign government. Because forfaiting may be done either with or without recourse to the exporter, the specific arrangements should be verified by the exporter.

Confirming is a financial service in which an independent company confirms an export order in the seller's country and makes payment for the goods in the currency of that country. Among the items eligible for confirmation (and thereby eligible for credit terms) are the goods themselves; inland, air, and ocean transportation costs; forwarding fees; custom brokerage fees; and duties. For the exporter, confirming means that the entire export transaction from plant to end user can be fully coordinated and paid for over time. Although confirming is common in Europe, it is still in its infancy in the United States. These three financing options are less frequently encountered and less widely available than commercial bank financing. Nevertheless, where offered locally, they help fill a financing gap for exporters.

8.3.2. Buyers and Suppliers

Foreign buyers of capital goods may make down payments that reduce the need for financing from other sources. In addition, buyers may make progress payments as the goods are completed, which also reduce other financing requirements. Letters of credit that allow for progress payments upon inspection by the buyer's agent or receipt of a statement by the exporter that a certain percentage of the product has been completed are not uncommon. In addition, suppliers may be willing to offer terms to the exporter if they are comfortable that they will receive payment.

Suppliers may be willing to accept assignment of a part of the proceeds of a letter of credit or a partial transfer of a transferable letter of credit. However, some banks allow only a single transfer or assignment of a letter of credit. Therefore, the exporter should investigate the policy of the bank that will be advising or confirming the letter of credit.

8.3.3. Pre-export Financing

There are many programmes which enable lenders to provide financing an exporter needs to purchase or produce a product for export, as well as finance short-term accounts receivable. Such programmes, can be used either to support ongoing export sales or to meet a temporary cash flow demand arising from a single export transaction. The loan principal can be up to 100 percent of the value of the collateral put up by the exporter, a relatively generous percentage. Eligible collateral includes foreign receivables, exportable inventory purchased with the proceeds of the loan, and goods in production. The term of the guaranteed line of credit is generally one year, but a longer period of renewals may be arranged.

8.3.4. Post-export Financing

There are banks which offer commercial and political risk insurance. Under the majority of policies, the insurance protects short-term credit extended for the sale of consumer goods, raw materials, commodities, spare parts, and other items normally sold on terms of up to 180 days. If the buyer fail to pay, banks reimburse the exporter in accordance with the terms of the policy.

In keeping with insurance principals, banks seek a reasonable spread of risk among the different export markets and avoids unduly concentrated credit exposure. Several private companies also offer export credit insurance covering political and commercial risks. Private insurance is available for established exporters with a proven track record, often at competitive premium rates, although underwriting capacity in particular markets may be limited. Coverage for contract repudiation and wrongful calling of a bid or performance bond may also be available in the private market.

8.3.5. Multilateral Development Banks (MDBs)

The Multilateral Development Banks (MDBs) are international financial institutuins owned by member governments. Their individual and collective objective is to promote economic and social progress in their developing member countries. The MDBs achieve this objective by providing loans, technical cooperation, grants, capital investment, and other types of assistance to governments, government agencies, and other entities in their developing member countries.

8.3.6. State and Local Export Finance Programmes

Several cities and states have funded and operate export financing programmes, including preshipment and postshipment working capital loans and guarantees, accounts receivable financing, and export insurance. To be eligible for these programmes, an export sale must generally be made under a letter of credit or with credit insurance coverage. A certain percentage of state or local content may also be required. However, some programmes may require only that certain facilities, such as a state or local port, be used; therefore, exporters may have several options.

9

HOW TO SHIP MY PRODUCT

When shipping a product overseas, the exporter must be aware of packing, labelling, documentation, and insurance requirements. It is important that exporters ensure that the merchandise is:

1. Packed correctly so that it arrives in good condition;
2. Labelled correctly to ensure that the goods are handled properly and arrive on time at the right place;
3. Documented correctly to meet government requirements, as well as proper collection standards; and
4. Insured against damage, loss, pilferage and delay.

Most exporters rely on an international freight forwarder to perform these services because of the multitude of considerations involved in physically exporting goods.

9.1 FREIGHT FORWARDERS

An international freight forwarder is an agent for the exporter in moving cargo to an overseas destination. These agents are familiar with the import rules and regulations of foreign countries, the export regulations of the government, the methods of shipping, and the documents related to foreign trade. Export freight forwarders are licensed by the International Air Transport Association (IATA) to handle air freight and the Federal Maritime Commission to handle ocean freight. Freight forwarders assist exporters in preparing price quotations by advising on freight costs, port charges, consular fees, costs of special documentation, insurance costs, and their handling fees.

They recommend the packing methods that will protect the merchandise during transit or can arrange to have the merchandise packed at the port or containerised. If the exporter prefers, freight forwarders can reserve the necessary space on a vessel, aircraft, train, or truck. The cost for their services is a legitimate export cost that should be included in the price charged to the customer. Once the order is ready for shipment, freight forwarders should be review all documents to ensure that everything is in order. This is of particular importance with letter of credit payment terms.

They may also prepare the bill of lading and any special required documentation. After shipment, they can route the documents to the seller, the buyer, or to a paying bank. Freight forwarders can also make arrangements with customs brokers overseas to ensure that the goods comply with customs export documentation regulations.

A customs broker is an individual or company that is licensed to transact customs business on behalf of others. Customs business is limited to those activities involving transactions related to the entry and admissibility of merchandise; its classification and valuation; the payment of duties, taxes, or other charges assessed or collected; or the refund, rebate, or drawback thereof.

9.2. PACKING

Exporters should be aware of the demands that international shipping puts on packaged goods. Exporters should jeep four potential problems in mind when designing an export shipping crate: breakage, moisture, pilferage and excess weight. Generally, cargo is carried in containers, but sometimes it is still shipped as breakbulk cargo. Besides the normal handling encountered in domestic transportation, a breakbulk shipment transported by ocean freight may be loaded aboard vessels in a net or by a sling, conveyor, or chute, that puts an added strain on the package.

During the voyage, goods may be stacked on top of or come into violent contact with other goods. Overseas, handling facilities may be less sophisticated than in the United States and the cargo could be dragged, pushed, rolled, or dropped during unloading, while moving through customs, or in transit to the final destination. Moisture is a constant concern because condensation may develop in the hold of a ship even if it is equipped with air conditioning and a dehumidifier.

Another aspect of this problem is that cargo may also be unloaded in precipitation, or the foreign port may not have covered storage facilities. Theft and pilferage are added risks. Buyers are often familiar with the port systems overseas, so they will often specify packaging requirements. If the buyer does not specify this, be sure the goods are prepared using these guidelines:

1. Pack in strong containers, adequately sealed and filled when possible.
2. To provide proper bracing in the container, regardless of size, make sure the weight is evenly distributed.
3. Goods should be palletised and when possible containerised.

4. Packages and packing filler should be made of moisture-resistant material.
5. To avoid pilferage, avoid writing contents or brand names on packages. Other safeguards include using straps, seals, and shrink wrapping.
6. Observe any product-specific hazardous materials packing requirements.

One popular method of shipment is to use containers obtained from carriers or private leasing companies. These containers vary in size, material, and construction and accommodate most cargo, but they are best suited for standard package sizes and shapes. Also, refrigerated and liquid bulk containers are usually readily available. Some containers are no more than semi-truck trailers lifted off their wheels, placed on a vessel at the port of export and then transferred to another set of wheels at the port of import. Normally, air shipments require less heavy packing than ocean shipments, though they should still be adequately protected, especially if they are highly pilferable.

In many instances, standard domestic packing is acceptable, especially if the product is durable and there is no concern for display packaging. In other instances, high-test cardboard or tri-wall construction boxes are more than adequate. Finally, because transportation costs are determined by volume and weight, specially reinforced and lightweight packing materials have been developed for exporting.

Packing goods to minimise volume and weight while reinforcing them may save money, as well as ensure that the goods are properly packed. It is recommended that a professional firm be hired to pack the products if the supplier is not equipped to do so. This service is usually provided at a moderate cost.

9.3. LABELLING

Specific marking and labelling is used on export shipping cartons and containers to:

1. Meet shipping regulations;
2. Ensure proper handling;
3. Conceal the identity of the contents;
4. Help receivers identify shipments; and
5. Insure compliance with environmental and safety standards.

The overseas buyer usually specifies which export marks should appear on the cargo for easy identification by receivers. Products can require many markings for shipment. For example, exporters need to put the following markings on cartons to be shipped:

1. Shipper's mark;
2. Country of origin:
3. Weight marking (in pounds and in kilograms);
4. Number of packages and size of cases (in inches and centimeters);
5. Handling marks (international pictorial symbols);
6. Cautionary markings, such as "This Side Up" or "Use No Hooks" (in English and in the language of the country of destination);
7. Port of entry;
8. Labels for hazardous materials (universal symbols adapted by the International Airi Transport Association and the International Maritime Organisation); and;
9. Ingredients (if applicable, also included in the language of the destination country).

Packages should be clearly marked to prevent misunderstandings and delays in shipping. Letters are generally stenciled onto packages and containers in waterproof ink. Markings should appear on three faces of the container, preferably on the top and on the two ends or the two sides. Ant old markings must be completely removed from previously used packaging. In addition to the port marks, the customer identification code, and an indication of origin, the marks should include the package number, gross and net weights, and dimensions.

If more than one package is being shipped, the total number of packages in the shipment should be included in the markings. The exporter should also add any special handling instructions. It is a good idea to repeat these instructions in the language of the country of destination and use standard international shipping and handling symbols. Customs regulations regarding freight labelling are strictly enforced. For example, many countries require that the country of origin be clearly labelled on each imported package. Most freight forwarders and export packing specialists can supply the necessary information regarding specific regulations.

9.4. DOCUMENTATION

Exporters should seriously consider having the freight forwarder handle the formidable amount of documentation that exporting requires as forwarders are specialists in this process. The following documents are commonly used in exporting; but which of them are necessary in a particular transaction depends on the requirements of the government and the government of the importing country. Air freight shipments are handled by air waybills, which can never be made in negotiable form.

A bill of lading is a contract between the owner of the goods and the carrier (as with domestic shipments). For vessels, there are two types: a straight bill of lading which is non-negotiable and a negotiable or shipper's order bill of lading. The latter can be bought, sold, or traded while the goods are in transit. The customer usually needs an original as proof of ownership to take possession of the goods. A commercial invoice is a bill for the goods from the seller to the buyer. These invoices are often used by governments to determine the true value of goods when assessing customs duties.

Governments that use the commercial invoice to control imports will often specify its form, content, number of copies, language to be used, and other characteristics. A consular invoice is a document that is required in some countries. It describes the shipment of goods and shows information such as the consignor, consignee, and value of the shipment. Certified by the consular official of the foreign country stationed here, it is used by the country's customs officials to verify the value, quantity, and nature of the shipment.

A certificate of origin is a document that is required in certain nations. It is a signed statement as to the origin of the export item. Certificate of origin are usually signed through a semiofficial organisation, such as a local chamber of commerce. A certificate may still be required even if the commercial invoice contains the information.

Inspection certification is required by some purchasers and countries in order to attest to the specifications of the goods shipped. This is usually performed by a third party and often obtained from independent testing organisations. A dock receipt and a warehouse receipt are used to transfer accountability when the export item is moved by the domestic carrier to the port of embarkation and left with the ship line for export. A destination control statement appears on the commercial invoice, and ocean or air waybill of lading to notify the carrier and all foreign parties that the item can be exported only to certain destinations.

An export license is a government document that authorises the export of specific goods in specific quantities to a particular destination. An export packing list considerably more detailed and informative than a standard domestic packing list. It an itemises the material in each individual package and indicates the type of package, such as a box, crate, drum, or carton. It also shows the individual net, legal, tare, and gross weights and measurements for each package.

Documentation must be precise because slight discrepancies or omissions may prevent merchandise from being exported, result in nonpayment, or even result in the seizure of the exporter's goods. Collection documents are subject to precise time limits and may not be honoured by a bank if the time has expired. Most documentation is routine for freight forwarders and customs brokers, but the exporter is ultimately responsible for the accuracy of its documents. The number and kind of documents the exporter must deal with varies depending on the destination of the shipment. Because each country has different import regulations, the exporter must be careful to provide all proper documentation.

9.5. SHIPPING

The handling of transportation is similar for domestic and export orders. Export marks are added to the standard information on a domestic bill of lading. These marks show the name of the exporting carrier and the latest allowed arrival date at the port of export. Instructions for the inland carrier to notify the international freight forwarder by telephone upon arrival should also be included. Exporters may find it useful to consult with a freight forwarder when determining the method of international shipping. Since carriers are often used for large and bulky shipments, the exporter should reserve space on the carrier well before actual shipment date. This reservation is called the booking contract.

International shipments are increasingly made on a through bill of lading under a multimodal contract. The multimodal transit operator (frequently one of the transporters) takes charge of and responsibility for the entire movement from factory to final destination. The cost of the shipment, the delivery schedule, and the accessibility to the shipped product by the foreign buyer are all factors to consider when determining the method of international shipping. Although air carriers can be more expensive, their cost may be offset by lower domestic shipping costs and quicker delivery times. These factors may give the exporter an edge over other competitors.

9.6. MARINE CARGO INSURANCE

Damaging weather conditions, rough handling by carriers, and other common hazards to cargo make insurance an important protection for exporters. If the terms of sale make the exporter responsible for insurance, the exporter should either obtain its own policy or insure the cargo under a freight forwarder's policy for a fee. If the terms of sale make the foreign buyer responsible, the exporter should not assume that adequate insurance has been obtained. If the buyer neglects to obtain adequate coverage, damage to the cargo may cause a major financial loss to the exporter.

Shipments by sea are covered by marine cargo insurance. Air shipments may also be covered by marine cargo insurance or insurance may be purchased from the air carrier. Export shipments are usually insured against loss, damage, and delay in transit by cargo insurance. Carrier liability is frequently limited by international agreements. Additionally, the coverage is substantially different from domestic coverage.

Arrangements for insurance may be made by either the buyer or the seller, in accordance with the terms of sale. Exporters are advised to consult with international insurance carriers or freight forwarders for more information. Although sellers and buyers can agree to different components, coverage is usually placed at 110 percent of the CIF (cost, insurance, freight) or CIP (carriage and insurance paid to) value.

9.7. EFFECTS OF TARIFFS

Finally, it is very important to consider the effects of tariffs, port handling fees, and taxes when determining your product's final cost as they can be high. Typically, the importer pays these charges. However, these costs will influence how much the buyer is willing to pay for your product.

9.8. CRITICAL ELEMENTS IN SELLING A PRODUCT

Proper pricing, complete and accurate quotations, choosing the terms of the sale, and selecting the payment method are four critical elements in selling a product or service overseas. Of the four, pricing can be the most problematic, even for an experienced exporter.

The price considerations listed below will help an exporter determine the best price for the product overseas.

— At what price should the firm sell its product in the foreign market?

— What type of market positioning (customer perception) does the company want to convey from its pricing structure?
— Does the export price reflect the product's quality?
— Is the price competitive?
— Should the firm pursue market penetration or market-skimming pricing objectives abroad?
— What type of discount (trade, cash, quantity) and allowances (advertising, trade-off) should the firm offer its foreign customers?
— Should prices differ by market segment?
— What should the firm do about product line pricing?
— What pricing options are available if the firm's costs increase or decrease? Is the demand in the foreign market elastic or inelastic?
— Are the prices going to be viewed by the foreign government as reasonable or exploitative?
— Do the foreign country's antidumping laws pose a problem?

As in the domestic market, the price at which a product or service is sold directly determines a firm's revenues. It is essential that a firm's market research include an evaluation of all of the variables that may affect the price range for the product or service. If a firm's price is too high, the product or service will not sell. If the price is too low, export activities may not be sufficiently profitable or may actually create a net loss. The traditional components of determining proper pricing are costs, market demand, and competition.

Each of these must be compared with the firm's objective in entering the foreign market. An analysis of each component from an export perspective may result in export prices that are different from domestic prices. It is also very important that the exporter take into account additional costs that are typically borne by the importer. They include tariffs, customs fees, currency fluctuation transaction costs and value-added taxes (VATs). These additional costs can add substantially to the final price paid by the importer, sometimes resulting in a total of more than double the domestic price.

9.9. MARKET OBJECTIVES

An important aspect of a company's pricing analysis is determining market objectives. For example, is the company attempting to penetrate a new market, looking for long-term market growth, or looking for an outlet for surplus production or outmoded products? Many firms view the foreign market as a secondary market and consequently have lower expectations regarding market share and sales volume. This naturally affects pricing decisions. Marketing and pricing objectives may be general or tailored to particular foreign markets.

The computation of the actual cost of producing a product and bringing it to market is the core element in determining if exporting is financially viable. Many new exporters calculate their export price by the cost-plus method. In the cost-plus method of calculation, the exporter starts with the domestic manufacturing cost and adds administration, research and development, overhead, freight forwarding, distributor margins, customs charges, and profit. The effect of this pricing approach may be that the export price escalates into an uncompetitive range.

Marginal cost pricing is a more competitive method of pricing a product for market entry. This method considers the direct, out-of-pocket expenses of producing and selling products for export as a floor beneath which prices cannot be set without incurring a loss. For example, additional costs may occur due to product modification for the export market that accommodates different sizes, electrical systems, or labels. On the other hand, costs may decrease if the export products are stripped-down versions or made without increasing the fixed costs of domestic production. Other costs should be assessed for domestic and export products according to how much benefit each product receives from such expenditures.

For most consumer goods, per capita income is a good gauge of a market's ability to pay. Some products may create such a strong demand such as popular goods like Levis, that even low per capita income will not affect their selling price. Simplifying the product to reduce its selling price may be an answer for the exporter to most lower per capita income markets. The firm must also keep in mind that currency fluctuations may alter the affordability of its goods. The firm should anticipate the type of potential customers. If the firm's primary customers in a developing country are expatriates or belong to the upper class, a higher price might be feasible even if the average per capita income is low.

9.10. COMPETITION IN EXPORT MARKET

In the domestic market, few companies are free to set prices without carefully evaluating their competitors' pricing policies. This situation is true in exporting, and is further complicated by the need to evaluate the competition's prices in each potential export market. If there are many competitors within the foreign market, the exporter may have little choice but to match the market price or even underprice the product or service in order to establish a market share. On the other hand, if the product or service is new to a particular foreign market, it may actually be possible to set a higher price than in the domestic market.

Many export transactions, particularly initial export transactions, begin with the receipt of an inquiry from abroad that is followed by a request for a quotation. The preferred method for export is a pro form a invoice, which is a quotation prepared in invoice format. A quotation describes the product, states a price for it, sets the time of shipment, and specifies the terms of the sale and terms of the payment. Since the foreign buyer may not be familiar with the product, the description of it in an overseas quotation usually must be more detailed than in a domestic quotation. The description should include the following points:

1. Seller's and buyer's names and addresses.
2. Buyer's reference number and date of inquiry.
3. Listing of requested products and brief description.
4. Price of each item
5. Appropriate gross and net shipping weight (in metric units where appropriate).
6. Appropriate total cubic volume and dimensions packed for export.
7. Trade discount.
8. Delivery point.
9. Terms of sale.
10. Terms of payment.
11. Insurance and shipping costs.
12. Validity period for quotation.
13. Total charges to be paid by customer.
14. Estimated shipping date from port or airport.
15. Currency of sale.

In addition to the points mentioned above, a pro forma invoice should include two statements. One that certifies the pro forma invoice is true and correct and another that gives the country of origin of the goods. The invoice should also be clearly marked "pro forma invoice." Pro forma invoices are models that the buyer uses when applying for an import license, opening a letter of credit or arranging for funds.

In fact, it is a good practice to include a pro forma invoice with any international quotation, regardless of whether it has been requested or not. If a specific price is agreed upon or guaranteed by the exporter, the precise period during which the offer remains valid should be specified. Additionally, it is very important that price quotations state explicitly that they are subject to change without notice.

10

OVERSEAS EXPORT/IMPORT STRUCTURE

Successful exporters start selling internationally by responding to an inquiry from a foreign firm. Thousands of firms receive such requests annually, but most firms do not become successful exporters. Generally, successful firms:

1. properly respond to inquiries;
2. conduct research on foreign customers;
3. differentiate between domestic and international sales;
4. build positive relationships with partners.

10.1 RESPONDING TO INQUIRY FROM A FOREIGN FIRM

Most but not all, foreign letters of inquiry are in English. A firm may look to certain service providers for assistance in translating a letter of inquiry in a foreign language. Colleges and universities are also an excellent source for translation. Most large cities have commercial translators who are hired on a fee-basis. Typically, a foreign firm will request product specifications, information, and price. Some inquiries will come directly from the end user, while other inquiries will come from distributors and agents who wish to sell the product in their market. A few foreign firms may already be familiar with the product and wish to immediately place an order. Regardless of the form such inquiries take, a firm should establish a policy to deal with them. Here are a few suggestions:

1. Expect some inquiries to have grammatical or typographical errors, which may result from the writer knowing English only as a second language. Secondly, printing standards differ outside the one country so do not consider the quality of the stationery as an indication of the wealth of the company. Despite first impressions, the inquiry may be from a reputable, well-established firm.
2. Reply promptly, completely, and clearly. The correspondent naturally wants to know something about the firm before a transaction takes place. The letter should introduce the firm sufficiently and establish it as a reliable supplier. The reply should provide a short, but adequate introduction to the firm, including bank references and other sources that confirm reliability. The firm's policy on exports should be stated, including cost, terms, and delivery. The firm may wish to respond with a pro forma invoice.
3. Enclose information on the firm's goods or services.
4. Send the reply airmail. Surface mail can take weeks or even months, whereas airmail usually takes only days. If a foreign firm's letter shows both a street address and a post office box, write to the post office box. In countries where mail delivery is unreliable, many firms prefer to have mail sent to the post office box.
5. If the company needs to meet a deadline, send the information via fax. Unlike telephone communications, fax may be used effectively despite differences in time zones and languages.

6. Set up a file for foreign letters. They may turn into definite prospects as export business grows. If the firm has an intermediary handling exports, the intermediary may use the file.

10.2 UNDERSTANDING POTENTIAL CLIENTS

There are many ways for a firm to research a foreign company before conducting any formal business. A company can save time and money by conducting basic research. These methods include:

1. *Business libraries*. Several private sector publications list and qualify international firms. There are also many regional and country directories.
2. *International banks*. Bankers have access to vast amounts of information on foreign firms and are usually very willing to assist corporate customers.
3. *Foreign embassies*. The commercial (business) sections of most foreign embassies have directories of firms located in their countries.

10.3. INTERNATIONAL SELLING PRACTICES

1. *Companies should be aware of basic business practices that are paramount to successful international selling*. Because cultures vary, there is no single code by which to conduct business. These practices transcend culture barriers and will help the company conduct business overseas.
2. *Keep promises*. The biggest complaint from foreign importers about suppliers is failure to ship as promised. A first order is particularly important because it shapes the customer's image of a firm as a dependable or an undependable supplier.

3. *Be polite, courteous, and friendly.* However, it is important to avoid undue familiarity or slang. Some overseas firms feel that the usual brief business letter is lacking in courtesy.
4. Personally sign all letters. Form letters are not satisfactory.

10.4. BUILDING RELATIONSHIPS

Once a relationship has been established with an overseas customer, representative, or distributor, it is important that the exporter work on building and maintaining that relationship. Common courtesy should dictate business activity. The exporter should keep in mind that a foreign contact should be treated and served as well as a domestic contact. For example, the company should keep customers and contacts notified of all changes, including price, personnel, address, and phone numbers.

Because of distance, a contact can "age" quickly and cease to be useful unless communication is maintained. For many companies, monthly or quarterly visits should be made to customers or distributors. This commitment to the business relationship, although not absolutely necessary, ensures that both the company and the product maintain high visibility in the marketplace. If the exporting firm cannot afford such frequent travel, it may use fax, e-mail, and telephone to keep the working relationship active and up to date.

10.5. SERVICE DELIVERY

Service is the prompt delivery of the product. It is courteous sales personnel. It is a user or service manual modified to meet your customer's needs. It is ready access to a service facility. It is knowledgeable, cost-effective maintenance, repair, or replacement. Service is location. Service is dealer support.

Service varies by the product type, the quality of the product, the price of the product, and the distribution channel employed. For export products that require no service - such as food products, some consumer goods, and commercial disposables - the issue is resolved once distribution channels, quality criteria, and return policies have been identified. On the other hand, the characteristics of consumer durables and some consumables demand that service be available. For such products, service is a feature expected by the consumer. In fact, foreign buyers of industrial goods typically place service at the forefront of the criteria they evaluate when making a purchase decision.

All foreign markets are sophisticated, and each has its own expectations of suppliers and vendors manufacturers or distributors must therefore ensure that their service performance is comparable to that of the predominant competitors in the market. This level of performance is an important determinant in ensuring a reasonable competitive position, given the other factors of product quality, price, promotion, and delivery.

An exporting firm's strategy and market entry decision may dictate that it does not provide after-sale service. It may determine that its export objective is the single or multiple opportunistic entry into export markets. Although this approach may work in the short term, subsequent product offerings will be less successful as buyers recall the failure to provide expected levels of service. As a result, market development and sales expenditures may result in one-time sales.

Service is an important factor in the initial export sale and ongoing success of products in foreign markets. Firms have many options for the delivery of service to foreign buyers. A high-cost option - and the most inconvenient for the foreign retail, wholesale, commercial, or industrial buyer - is for the product to be returned to the manufacturing or distribution facility for service or repair. The buyer incurs a high cost and loses the use of the product for an extended period, while the seller must incur the export cost of the same product a second time to return it. Fortunately, there are practical, cost-effective alternatives to this approach.

If the selected export distribution channel is a joint venture or other partnership arrangement, the overseas partner may have a service or repair capability in the markets to be penetrated. An exporting firm's negotiations and agreements with its partner should include explicit provisions for repairs, maintenance, and warranty service. The cost of providing this service should be negotiated into the agreement. For goods sold at retail outlets, a preferred service option is to identify and use local service facilities. Though this requires up-front expenses to identify and train local service outlets, the costs are more than repaid in the long run.

There are administrative, training, and supervisory overhead costs associated with such a warranty and service programme. The benefit, however, is that the company is now perceived to be a local company that competes on equal footing with domestic manufacturers. Exporters should keep this example in mind when entering foreign markets.

Exporting a product into commercial or industrial markets may dictate a different approach. For the many companies that sell through distributors, selection of a representative to serve a region, a nation, or a market should be based not only on the distributing company's ability to sell effectively but also on its ability and willingness to service the product. Assessing that ability to service requires that the exporter ask questions about existing service facilities; about the types, models, and age of existing service equipment; about training practices for service personnel; and about the firm's experience in servicing similar products.

If the product being exported is to be sold directly to end users, service and timely performance are critical to success. The nature of the product may require delivery of on-site service to the buyer within very specific time parameters. These are negotiable issues for which the exporter must be prepared. Such on-site service may be available from service organisations in the buyer's country; or the exporting company may have to send personnel to the site to provide service. The sales contract should anticipate a reasonable level of on-site service and should include the associated costs. Existing performance and service history can serve as a guide for estimating service and warranty requirements on export sales, and sales can be costed accordingly. This practice is accepted by small and large exporters alike.

At some level of export activity, it may become cost-effective for a company to establish its own branch or subsidiary operation in the foreign market. The branch or subsidiary may be a one-person operation or a more extensive facility staffed with sales, administration, service, and other personnel, most of whom are local nationals in the market. This high-cost option enables the exporter to ensure sales and service quality, provided that personnel are trained in sales, products, and service on an ongoing basis. The benefits of this option include the control it gives to the exporter and the ability to serve multiple markets in a single region.

Manufacturers of similar or related products may find it cost-effective to consolidate service, training, and support in each export market. Service can be delivered by a personnel, a foreign facility under contract, or a jointly owned foreign-based service facility. Despite its cost benefits, this option raises a number of issues. Such joint activity may be interpreted as being in restraint of trade or otherwise market controlling or monopolistic. Exporters that are considering it should therefore obtain competent legal counsel when developing this joint operating arrangement. Exporters may wish to consider obtaining an export trade certificate of review, which provides limited immunity from antitrust laws.

Service is a very important part of many types of representation agreements. For better or worse, the quality of service in a country or region affects the manufacturer's reputation there. Quality of service also affects the intellectual property rights of the manufacturer. A trademark is a mark of source, with associated quality and performance. If quality control is not maintained, the manufacturer can lose its rights to the product, because one can argue that, within that foreign market, the manufacturer has abandoned the trademark to the distributor.

It is, therefore, imperative that agreements with a representative be specific about the form of the repair or service facility, the number of people on the staff, inspection provisions, training programmes, and payment of costs associated with maintaining a suitable facility. The depth or breadth of a warranty in a given country or region should be tied to the service facility to which the manufacturer has access in that market. It is important to promise only what can be delivered. Another part of the representative agreement may detail the training the exporter will provide to its foreign representative. This detail can include frequency of training, who must be trained, where the training is provided, and which party absorbs travel and per diem costs.

10.6. SALES OPPORTUNITIES

Foreign buyers typically have limited contact with the manufacturer or its personnel. The foreign service facility is, in fact, one of the major contact points between the exporter and the buyer. To a great extent, the manufacturer's reputation is made by the overseas service facility.

The service experience can be a positive and reinforcing sales and service encounter. It can also be an excellent sales opportunity if the service personnel are trained to take advantage of the situation. Service personnel can help the customer make life cycle decisions regarding the efficient operation of the product, how to update it for more and longer cost-effective operation, and when to replace it as the task expands or changes. Each service contact is an opportunity to educate the customer and expand the exporter's sales opportunities.

Service is also an important aspect of selling solutions and benefits rather than product features. More than one leading industrial products exporter sells its products as a "tool to do the job" rather than as a "truck" or a "cutting machine" or "software." Service capability enables customers to complete their jobs more efficiently with the exporter's "tool." Training service managers and personnel in this type of thinking vitalises service facilities and generates new sales opportunities.

Each foreign market offers a unique opportunity for the exporter. Care and attention to the development of in-country sales and distribution capabilities is paramount. Delivery of after-sales service is critical to the near- and long-term success of the company's efforts in any market. Senior personnel should commit to a programme of regular travel to each foreign market to meet with the company's representatives, clients, and others who are important to the success of the firm in that market.

The benefits of such a programme are twofold. First, executive management learns more about the foreign marketplace and the firm's capabilities. Second, the in-country representative appreciates the attention and understands the importance of the foreign market in the exporter's long-term plans. As a result, such visits help build a strong, productive relationship.

10.7. FINDING AN OVERSEAS REPRESENTATIVE

Once you've determined that you want to export directly, instead of indirectly, you must decide if you want to sell through an agent or a distributor. There is a substantial difference between the two categories both legally and functionally. It is often difficult and expensive to unwind from established relationships, therefore it is important to carefully determine the correct connection for your exporting efforts. Once this is made, you need to locate, select, screen, and reach an operating agreement with your contact.

A thorough analysis of your needs and requirements, as well as a comprehensive search, evaluation, and selection are critical to the success of your marketing effort. Remember, the time spent here is time well spent and the completeness of your search will reflect in the performance of your export programme.

The decision whether to use a distributor or an agent is a substantial one and vital to the nature of your overseas efforts. The success or failure of your export effort will depend upon this decision. Consultation with your legal counsel, the practicalities of your export requirements, and the traditions of the country you are exporting to will have substantial bearing on your decision. The time and effort spent up front in your evaluation and determination of the correct avenue will greatly benefit the success of your export programme.

Representation of any kind in a foreign country is much like a marriage, it can be easy to get into but often difficult and expensive to terminate. If you are not confident in your selection of a representative, sell directly to retailers or other end users until the right one is located.

Use an agent if:

1. It is the accepted distribution method in the country you are exporting to.
2. You do not need to maintain inventory in the foreign country. For example, if you manufacture custom or capital equipment, sell services, or can have inventory shipped direct for individual orders, you probably do not need to keep stock and maintain a distributorship programme in the foreign country.
3. You want to maintain direct control of the sales of your products overseas. Since agents sell the product on behalf of the exporter, they must sell it at the exporter's price, under specified conditions, and with prescribed representations.
4. You intend to benefit from corporate identity and intend to conduct business under your own name.

Use a distributor if:

1. It is the accepted distribution method in the country to which you are exporting.
2. You need to maintain inventory on the foreign country and do not want to maintain your own distribution network.

10.8.1. Private Agencies and Sources

Existing business relationships and associations provide another avenue to making export connections and obtaining leads. These include:

1. *Banks and other Financial Institutions:* Most larger banks and financial institutions are now multinational, have correspondent relationships

with overseas counterparts, or maintain a department to handle foreign financial transactions. These can frequently provide leads and introductions to overseas markets.

2. *Business Colleagues:* Business colleagues with existing relationships and first-hand experience may give personal recommendation or introductions to prospective representatives, buyers, or distributors.
3. *Trade and Industry Associations:* Trade and industry associations are an excellent opportunity to share information and contacts with those having similar interests and contacts.
4. *Trade Shows and Missions:* Trade shows and missions are one of the best ways to not only share information with other exporters, but provide the opportunity for direct contact with interested buyers, representatives, distributors.
5. *Export Seminars:* Seminars oriented towards exporting offer yet another opportunity to meet like-minded and experienced producers as well as develop additional expertise.
6. *Miscellaneous Contacts:* Many times contacts can be made through unexpected sources such as freight carriers, shipping agents, airlines, commodities brokers, port authorities, and others can be a valuable source of information, contacts, and leads.
7. *Electronic Resources and Other Media*: Current technology enhances the distributor search effort by giving you access to the Internet and World Wide Web. Several programmes can be accessed through the Web and will be instrumental in your search. You may also have some success using directories at a library with an extensive international business section. Have the librarian locate directories of

importers for the specific countries you are interested in and scan them for products for your particular industry.

10.8.2. Contacting Potential Representatives

Having obtained a list of contacts of potential representatives, the next step is to establish contact to determine those who might be available and have interest in acting in that capacity. The best method is the face to face contact which is available during trade shows, trade missions, and foreign travel. If this is not practical, communicate through written correspondence. Contact representatives through letters, telephone or telefax, cables, or for many, through the electronic medium.

10.8.3. Evaluating Potential Representatives

The arrangements you make with your representative are critical to the success of your marketing efforts. Too little care in evaluating and selecting your representative may be regretted later. You want to know as much as possible about your contacts to make informed decisions and assure mutual compatibility. At a minimum, you should consult the following information when available:

10.8.3.1. Background Information on the Representative

The more information available to you on a prospective representative, the better. At a minimum, you should inquire about the following:

— Company letterhead,

— History and experience, particularly with similar products or industry,

— Qualifications of principals and/or officers,

— Adequacy of personnel, facilities, and resources,

— Availability of the resources to meet your requirements,

— Current sales volume and size of inventories,

— Territories they cover,

— Product lines they carry,

— Customer base,

— Current clients,

— Past performance,

— Familiarity with business practices,

— Nature of sales force,

— Media resources.

10.8.3.2. Third Party Evaluations

Often, evaluations are made by independent companies and agencies.

10.8.3.3. Bank and Trade References

The relationship a contact has with his bank, as well as the extent and nature of credit availability, types of accounts, and history, are often indicative of the prospect's business practices and history. Additionally, trade contacts such as suppliers, shipping agents, customs brokers, etc. can provide valuable background regarding the history, strength, integrity, and reliability of the contact.

10.8.3.4. Current Business References

One of the best ways to explore how you might expect a relationship to proceed can be indicated by those your prospective representative has current business relationships. These can be other exporters currently utilising this source, accountants and legal firms, and industry and trade associations.

10.8.3.5. Commercial Credit Reports

Credit reports are often available from commercial sources. They can provide information regarding your contact's financial strength, payment histories, and other relevant financial data.

10.8.3.6. Draft and Execute Agreements

After selecting your representative, the next step is to draft and execute a definitive contract or agreement which will serve as a basis of documenting your understandings and responsibilities. This must be done in concert with your legal counsel due to its importance to the relationship with your representative and your legal liabilities.

As a general rule, the following items should be included in every agreement:

— Names, addresses, nature and relationship of parties,
— Product description,
— Definition of territory,
— Exclusivity conditions,
— Basis for compensation,
— Product pricing agreements,
— Sales goals and market share expectations,
— Nontransferability of assigned rights,
— Confidentiality agreements and understandings regarding prohibitions in dealing with competing products,
— Jurisdiction regarding agreements and their enforcement,

— Responsibilities for advertising, ordering, inventories and delivery, maintenance, warranty work, and other relevant operating concerns,

— Term of the agreement and provisions for modification, cancellation, extensions, or renewal.

Consultation with your legal counsel is critical in any written contract. Since legal systems, customs, and regulations differ throughout the world, co-counsel knowledgeable in the practices of the foreign country may also be necessary. Contracts and agreements can be quite extensive but must be as thorough as possible to preclude misinterpretation of intent and subsequent controversy. Due to the dynamics of relationships as well as marketplaces and global politics, modifications will probably be required over the life of the agreement and you should be prepared for that necessity.

SUGGESTED READINGS

Felleisen, Matthias and Daniel P. Friedman. (1986). "A closer look at export and import statements." *Journal of Computer Languages* 11(1): 29—37.

Hill, McGraw. (1996). *A Basic Guide To Importing by U.S. Customs Service.*

International Chamber of Commerce. (1999). *Incoterms 2000: ICC Official Rules for the Interpretation of Trade Terms.* ICC Publishing.

Jagoe, John R. "Export Sales and Marketing Manual." Export USA Publications.

Johnson, Thomas E. (2002). *Export/import procedures and documentation.* New York: AMACOM.

Nelson Wiley, Carl A. (2002). *Import/Export: How to Get Started in International Trade.*

United States Custom Service Books For Business. (2003). *Importing Into the United States: A Guide for Commercial Importers.*

Weiss Wiley, Kenneth D. (2002). *Building an Import/Export Business.*